IRISH WISDOM

PRESERVED IN BIBLE

AND PYRAMIDS

(1923)

Partial Contents: The Problem of the Pyramids; The Struggle between Rome and Eire; The Bible an Irish Book Altered and Adapted by British-Roman Transcribers; The Irish Pope-Kings Formerly the Rulers of Britain; Rome and the Pagans; Hebrew a Sacerdotal Dialect Improvised from the Irish Language for the Secret Use of the Priests; Going into Egypt; The Four-Pyramid Group and Sphinx, Designed and Erected to Symbolize Man; The Mystery of the Sphinx and the Problem Solved; The Great Pyramid of Iesa.

Conor MacDari

ISBN 1-56459-754-7

IRISH WISDOM

By CONOR MacDARI

A NEW and interesting version of ancient history is unfolded here for the first time. The author has made a deep study of his subject, presenting the whole in a thorough and interesting manner, and revealing much that is new. These pages will go far in helping one obtain a clear perspective of the past.

The author starts with the origin of the Great Pyramid, calling it "the companion piece of the Bible—the one in art, the other in literature," and explains the reasons for its existence, its message and significance. He then traces history from the time of the ancient Phoenicians through the Roman era, showing what part the Irish race took in these important times.

Such interesting topics as "The struggle between Rome and Eire," "The Bible an Irish Book," "The Irish Pope-Kings formerly the Rulers of Britain," "Hebrew a Sacerdotal Dialect improvised from the Irish Language," etc., are fully discussed by the author. Not only those interested in Irish history will profit by reading this book, but all who are interested in the ancient history of the world will find the volume worthy of serious consideration.

PREFACE

In offering these pages to the public I am in accord with a sentiment which is universal, at least I believe among enlightened minds, and that is the desire to know the truth of history instead of the fiction which has been substituted therefor. In these pages I have drawn aside the veil with which true history has been hidden, besides disclosing what agencies perpetrated this great deception and their reasons for so doing; thereby I enable the reader to obtain a clear perspective of the past.

The Muse of History has had no official chronicler to record the events of mankind and preserve them intact for the inspection of posterity. Instead, the field has been preëmpted and exploited by powerful and selfish interests who have falsified history to an outrageous extent. During a former age a system of records and a chronicle of events came down to us until a comparatively recent time, historically speaking, which gave a true account and a just portrayal of life in those ancient times. The reason for this was that it was the natural and obvious result of a static or settled state of society which lasted for thousands of years, and there was no object or purpose in concealment.

During those ages the intellectual powers had full play, and the individual man reached a higher plane poetically, philosophically and spiritually than at any other period in the World's history. This may be rightly called the Celtic Cultural Age. To this age we may look back as the source from which we obtained the great gifts which we of today esteem as of the most priceless value to mankind.

The causes inherent in man and society which brought about a change from this ancient social state, resulting in the suppression of the history of those times and the substitution therefor of a mass of fiction, are told for the first time in these pages. I might easily have enlarged this little volume; in fact it was with difficulty that I was enabled to keep it within its present compressed form. To enlarge upon or to extend some of the topics treated herein, such as the Bible, would require a very large volume or series of volumes in themselves.

However, I hope that I have given out enough of truth in this work to interest or to help everyone into whose hands it may come. Believing this to be so, I send it forth to go from man to man like a messenger to deliver its message of Light and Truth.

THE AUTHOR

CONTENTS

v

CONTENTS

IRISH WISDOM PRESERVED IN BIBLE AND PYRAMIDS

CHAPTER I

THE PROBLEM OF THE PYRAMIDS

THE solution of the mystery of the pyramids of Egypt has been a problem which has not only puzzled mankind in general during the ages of the past, but which has, as well, mystified the minds of scholars and thinkers even to this our present day. For, excepting the select few who were initiates of the ancient priesthood to whom it was a carefully guarded secret, no others knew or understood its full import and significance.

The Great Pyramid in its original and dazzling splendor of light under the Egyptian Sun was the object of wonderment and awe to all beholders. It surpassed in sublime grandeur any other monument or structure ever erected by man on this globe. It was considered the greatest of the seven wonders of the ancient world. Its partial destruction and defacement by removing its upper part and capstone, and by stripping it of its outer casing of white stone which gave to it an aspect of dazzling brightness, leaving it in outward appearance bare and nude, silent and mute as to its mission, as a milestone without a figure, — this has been a great loss to mankind. In its former glory it was a mountain of light, a blaze of brightness, a symbol in the desert. It was a testimonial in living stone, bespeaking to mankind of their inheritance in a spiritual kingdom. At noonday its lofty, golden capstone seemed to be at one with the Sun, uniting Earth and Heaven in eternal unity, a symbolic union of Spirit and Matter. To mar this sublime Pillar, this grand masterpiece of the Irish Magian priests of Iesa, was a part of a plot as selfish as any ever conceived.

It was conceived and put into effect by the ruling spirits at the head of the Roman Church and State of their day, who cherished the ambitious and far-reaching idea of nothing less than universal rule for their Church and Empire.

In the course of these pages, I will endeavor to explain and expose the conspiracy and the means by which those designing men who composed it advanced their project. And, with the aid of their successors, they, I purpose to show, by persistent effort, brought the greater part of the western world under their Empire and Church dominion, and brought this conspiracy to an almost complete success.

It was the idea held by the leaders of the Roman Church and State (they were practically one) that all power should be centralized in the head of the Church who was also Emperor of The State. And any and all religious institutions which in any way conflicted with this idea were to be done away with. For this reason, the mystery cults were suppressed and initiation into the ancient or esoteric mysteries were forbidden, so that no religious establishment, worship, or practice would exist which would draw and hold men to it other than the Roman State Church. And, besides, as the study and preparation necessary for those who were selected for initiation into the higher mysteries was such as to develop a highly philosophic and spiritual state of mind, such study and preparation did not comport with the object which the Church rulers had in view. Such minds would not yield adherence to a mere political and idolatrous church whose doctrines were, in the main, intended for the uninstructed multitude. Such minds could not be dominated by a political or mercenary priesthood. They were enlightened men and they stood in the way of the Church project. Therefore, the institutions which produced such men were to be suppressed.

The Great Pyramid of Iesa was used as a Temple of Initiation for inculcating the mysteries of nature and the occult powers of the soul. The decree of the Church and the execution of its policy to close The Great Pyramid Temple and suppress its institution practically put an end to the development of enlightened minds in the Nile valley. The way was then clear for the unopposed spread of superstition and cruel fanaticism among the masses. With the Great Pyramid closed, its passages filled up with stone and rubbish, its initiate priests banished, the way was paved for the long night of darkness and ignorance which followed and which is known in history as the Dark Ages.

These were the conditions which were best suited for the political Church of Rome to take root and flourish in, and wherever she flourishes today such conditions are more or less present.

During the Dark Ages, intercourse between the countries of western Europe and the East was meager, and interest in the pyramids was mostly held by the few who happened to be enlightened enough to know of their existence, as education was not as general at that time as it is today; it was mostly confined to small castes, even in the so-called enlightened countries.

Since the Napoleonic expedition to Egypt in the early part of the nineteenth century, and because of the accounts brought back by those Savants who were members of that expeditionary force, an intense interest was awakened in France, Germany, and particularly England, where a hot controversy raged for many years between the advocates of different theories as to when the pyramids were built, for what purpose, and who their builders were. All this resulted in the creation among the enlightened class of what was practically a Pyramid Cult. This Cult succeeded in spreading its views from this British center to all other countries. It all served to bring about an intense interest in The Great Pyramid and caused an almost endless speculation as to its erection and use.

Some held that it was built as a place of worship, others that it was built for a granary, a place of refuge in time of danger or of flood, a tomb for a king, or merely as a caprice or whim of a ruler to keep the people employed. The idea was also advanced that the pyramids and obelisks were built as a part of a system for the measuring of time by the length of the shadow they cast, and for determining the length of the seasons and the proper time for planting. Some of these speculations were as specious and far-fetched as others were ingenious.

But all to vain purpose. Deep thinkers could not quite accept the prevailing opinions, although none came forward with a solution of the problem. From the nature of the task, we know now that it was too difficult for any individual researcher to accomplish in a short time, especially during the distraction of a controversy. The proofs were cryptic and were hidden too deeply behind a smoke screen of false history and myth to be easily discovered. It required time to analyze and examine the evidence and to sift the true from the false. This we have been able to do with the aid of those who have gone before us.

However, the whole controversy served to arouse an intensified interest, such as has been awakened among scholars and thinkers everywhere in The Great Pyramid — this companion piece of the Bible — the one in art, the other in literature. The Bible is the "Word" in script, The Great Pyramid is the "Word" in stone, and both came from the same source, the Irish Magian priesthood of Iesa.

The interest in this great structure has been stimulated, especially during the last fifty years, since the increase of travel and the wide circulation of books and the descriptions of travelers. Through this means has interest been kept alive and a desire to know the history and secrets concerning those most curious and mysterious

monuments of the past to which we are heirs. The fact
that the solution of the problem of the pyramids was
not given out to the world before now is no proof in itself
that this knowledge did not exist.

It is my belief that it was always known and in the
possession of the ruling spirits of the Church of Rome and
the High Priests of the Church of England. The success
of the former institution was dependent upon the suppression of this knowledge. But it was, and it is up to
this day, also one of the most jealously guarded secrets
of the High Church of England. Otherwise, this
knowledge could not but be widely known as the evidence
is so plain that it is only through a studied and agreed
upon silence that the facts have been kept from becoming
common knowledge. The Great Pyramid and the
group of which it is the premier, together with the
temples of the Nile valley, are the most convincing
witnesses and testimonials, offering no chance for
contradiction or uncertainty, as to the accomplishments
and genius of the Irish, or, as it is called in history, the
Aryan Race.

In their great missionary pilgrimage they circled the
globe in order to give religion and a knowledge of God
to the different races of mankind. They also established
priesthoods and gave alphabets to the races who were
unenlightened in such matters up to that time. Ireland
is the country in which the arts and sciences were first
discovered and developed. To this country the Greeks
applied the term "Ogygia," a term which was never
given but to the very ancient; and it is from the Irish

(Aryans) that the Greeks traced their descent (Donnelly's *Atlantis*, p. 458).   To the Irish Magi we owe the discovery of fire and the common grains which they developed from the grasses.   They were the first people to practice agriculture; they invented the common tools of workmanship which have come down to us practically unchanged from those ancient times.

There is no mistaking the monuments left by the Irish who were once the rulers and masters of the whole earth. Their rule embraced all countries — it was world-wide. Ireland was the first mistress of the seas; it was the first and only world-wide empire which has ever been known.   For it was spiritual.   It was greater in extent than Persian, Greek, Roman, or Mogul ever attained to.   The remains of their works, wherever they are found, bear an unmistakable similarity in shape and character.   They are huge, immense, and conceived and carried out on a plan so extensive that it awes the mind of the man of today.   These remains extend from Ireland along the Atlantic coast of Europe to Africa, along the Mediterranean Sea to Egypt, India, China, Java, Tahiti, and the Caroline Islands in the South Pacific Ocean. On the American Continent we find the round tower near Newport, R. I., which bespeaks its Irish origin, and the great pyramidal mounds of the Ohio and Mississippi valleys; also the ruined temples of Yucatan and Mexico, and similar remains in South America are all evidences of their handiwork.   All owe their origin to the same source, and they establish beyond any doubt that the Irish were the first real discoverers of America and that

they established civilization on this western continent.
It was tradition founded on that fact which gave hope
and encouragement to later adventurers.

The very name of God among the Indians of our
country was an Irish name derived from those missionaries
and explorers centuries before Christopher
Columbus or Eric the Red were born. One of the Irish
names of God is Mann, and Manitha is the Irish word
for Holy. The Indian name for God was Manitou, the
Holy One. The Indians also had another name for
God, and this again was Irish. It was Manabasha, the
Sun God.* It is a compound word with the root word
Mann (Holy) and Basha (of the cows, the Bull — virtually
the same as Baal, the Irish Sun-God). So the
name signifies the Holy Life Giver, or Holy Creator.
Anyone who knows the Celtic tongue will recognize this
fact at once, and so will all competent students of
philology.

No one, after reading this treatise on The Great
Pyramid, will ever have a doubt as to who its authors
were or as to whether the high personages in England,
who always have assumed direction of the ship of state,
have had a knowledge of who the builders of The Great
Pyramid were. Nor will there be any doubt but that the
ruling spirits of the Church of Rome have had this
knowledge and that they still keep it a close secret.

*This was the name preserved by tradition among the Chippewas, according
to J. S. Kohl (quoted in *Atlantis*, p. 108), and it is the name
of the Man Saved from the Deluge. This seeming confusion of names as
to the identity of characters in the Deluge Legend need not seem strange,
as long periods of time work changes in the legends of all peoples.

It is high time this knowledge be given to the world and responsibility for its suppression be placed where it belongs. There has been maintained a smoke screen around Ireland since the English invasion and the consequent looting of the island with the destruction of her sacred shrines, which was meant to obscure her great past and her contribution to letters, science, culture, true religion, and civilization. It goes without saying that we owe more to ancient Eire for these blessings than to any other people or nation.

CHAPTER II

AN ELUCIDATION OF HISTORY

IN ancient times the ruler of the state, according to the extent of his power, dependent as to whether he was an overlord king, having subject kings as vassals, or being a subject king himself, held two offices jointly in his own person, that of king or emperor, and that of head of the church in his dominion.

The fact of his holding such autocratic power led to the assumption of attributes of divinity in order to hold the people in awe of him. The qualities of Divinity we have seen attributed to rulers in our day. In Russia, China, Japan, and, not so long ago, in England, the belief was held that any disease which would not yield to the treatment of a physician could be cured by a mere touch of the king's hand or even of his garment.

The head of the Irish State-Church held this supreme pontifical power in Europe until challenged first by Persia, then by Greece, and, later, by Rome, who, when a favorable time arrived for her to assert her independence, set up jointly a church and state for herself.

For, let it be known, Rome was at one time a colony of Ireland. The name Rome is a compound of two Irish words: Ro, meaning before, and Ome, meaning body, earth, or grave. But in its mythic meaning it is made to signify Before Heaven (Ro) and Earth (Ome), the two together meaning Heaven and Earth. Hence the "eternal" city Rome.

The river of Rome, the Tiber, also bears an Irish name. It derives its name from Tubber, the Irish word for a well or spring of water. Hence, the Tiber is the "Spring Water River." As the poet Longfellow truly says, "Their names are on your waters and ye may not wash them out."

The fact is that Ireland was the first power that colonized along both sides of the Mediterranean Sea, and, therefore, the colonies came from the West instead of from the East as our astute Roman and British historians would have us believe. And the world has believed it up to now. But the deception, when once exposed, is too clear for anyone to be deceived by it.

Investigators have followed the false clew sent out from this source and found nothing in the East to support this claim that the Aryans emigrated from the East and colonized towards the West. The real and true evidence points just in the opposite direction.

The *American Cyclopaedia*, Art. " Ethnology," (quoted in Donnelly's *Atlantis*) : says "Bonfrey, L. Geiger and other students of the ancient Indo-European languages have recently advanced the opinion that the original home of Indo-European races must be sought in Europe, because their stock of words is rich in the names of plants and animals, and contains names of seasons that are not found in tropical countries or anywhere else in Asia."

Max Muller says : "The nations who are comprehended under the common appellation of Indo-European

— the Hindoos, the Persians, the Celts, Germans, Romans, Greeks, and Slavs — do not only share the same words and the same grammar, slightly modified in each country, but they seem to have likewise preserved a mass of popular traditions which had grown up before they left their common home" (Donnelly's *Atlantis*, p. 458).

To obscure knowledge of this homeland and the reason for so doing have engaged the greatest organized propaganda for spreading misinformation that we have any knowledge of, as will become apparent in these pages.

We are told that the "Phoenicians" planted those colonies and that they came from the East, from the coasts of what is now Syria, or Phoenicia, as they say it was formerly called. Ireland is the homeland of the "Phoenicians," which word is a secret name for the insular race of mariners and traders who carried on commerce with the whole world. Sidon and Tyre are mythic names applied for purposes of deception to the two cities at the eastern end of the Mediterranean Sea. Sidon is an Irish word and means the hips or buttocks. Tyre means the earth or body, and the purple color or dye which, we are told, made this city famous is the blood which courses through the body. The coast of Syria was never suited to the needs of a seafaring race and such a race never developed there. But Ireland, an island indented with bays, loughs, and harbors, was suitable to the development of just such a race as we should expect to find there. For secret reasons the name "Phoenicians" was applied to *the Irish Race*. It is written purposely in this form of spelling which has served well in throwing people off the track and helped very well in keeping up the deception.

If they had written the word in its plain form of Finician, there would be too many who were liable to see the true meaning of it and, thereby, get a clew to the real truth which was meant to be concealed. The word Fion or Fin is an Irish name of the Sun, and the Finicians were the Irish Sun worshippers or the Magian priests of Iesa, the Irish Sun God, who brought their civilization and arts, already developed in Ireland, with them to Egypt. There they erected their monumental altars to the God of the Sun, of which The Great Pyramid was the crowning symbol and masterpiece. They carried their mission from there to the farther lands of the East.

Plain documentary evidence of the ordinary kind to prove these facts has been destroyed, but in their stead a secret system was adopted to preserve them or, rather, to conceal them from "profane" eyes. So that the facts can be attested to and proved in the most convincing manner by the aid of the covert or hidden allusions and by the secret code intended solely for the benefit of the "anointed few," the priesthood. But those monuments which they left behind, although now in ruins from vandal hands, speak most eloquently for them. They testify in most emphatic and convincing manner as to who their authors were. Their testimony is most pronounced and unimpeachable and puts to flight all false witnesses.

The Great Pyramid of Iesa, the Bible, and the Irish Language — through means of these aids we have been able to reveal the truth which had been buried beneath a mass of myth and fiction by the priests of Rome and their British collaborators. Honest, and we believe, impartial investigators have confessed themselves at a loss to account for the origin of Egypt's civilization with its arts and sciences. It did not seem like other things, there was such silence about it, and a mysterious absence of facts regarding its birth which was most puzzling. It did not appear to grow from small beginnings and gradually advance to a better and more perfect state by successive stages. It seemed as if it was so from the beginning. No trace of early beginnings could be found by investigators. Now, these are not the natural or usual features of a civilization which is native to any country or society.

Such a civilization as Egypt had could not be developed suddenly and come into being at once any more than an oak tree could spring from the acorn full grown, or that a great city could be naturally developed with all its varied institutions and arise in a single day. Many writers have noted this peculiarity about Egypt's history and her civilization without happening on to the key which would solve the puzzle. As they were not aware of the existence of a plot to conceal her history, they were not suspicious enough of the priests who wrote her history, as *they* would have us see it. Renan says of Egypt, "It has no archaic epoch." Donnelly says, "The carpenters' and masons' tools of the ancient Egyptians were almost identical with those used among us today." Taylor says (*Anthropology*, p. 192), "Among the ancient cultured nations of Egypt and Assyria handicrafts had already come to a stage which could only have been reached by thousands of years of progress. In museums still may be examined the work of their joiners, stone-cutters, goldsmiths, wonderful in skill and finish, and often putting to shame the modern artificer."

Osborn says, "It bursts upon us at once in the flower of its highest perfection."

Dr. Seis says (*A Miracle in Stone*, p. 40), "It suddenly takes its place in the world in all its matchless magnificence, without father, without mother and as clean apart from all evolution as if it had dropped from the unknown heavens."

We have already stated where it came from — Ireland and its Master Adepts. Reginald Stuart Poole says (*Contemporary Review*, August, 1881, p. 43, quoted by Donnelly), "When we consider the high ideal of the Egyptians, as proved by their portrayals of a just life, the principles they laid down as the basis of ethics, the elevation of women among them, their humanity in war, we must admit that their normal place ranks very high among the nations of antiquity."

They were just such a people as we would expect to find associated with and benignantly ruled by a pure and virtuous priesthood such as the Irish Magian priesthood undoubtedly was, else its priests would not have been chosen to be the instructors and elder brothers of the infant and backward races of that early day.

Rawlinson (*Origin of Nations*, p. 13) says, "Now, in Egypt, it is notorious that there is no indication of any early period of savagery or barbarism. All the authorities show that, however far back we go, we find in Egypt no rude or uncivilized time out of which civilization is developed — we see no barbarous customs, not even the habit, so slowly abandoned by all people, of wearing arms when not on military service."

" By their fruits shall ye know them."

Goodrich says, "Great and splendid as are the things which we know about oldest Egypt, she is made a thousand times more sublime by our uncertainty as to the limits of her accomplishments. — The effect of research seems to be to prove the objects of it to be much older than we thought them to be — some things thought to be wholly modern having been proved to be repetitions of things Egyptian, and other things known to have been Egyptian being by every advance in knowledge carried back more and more toward the beginning of things. She shakes our most rooted ideas concerning the world's history; she has not ceased to be a puzzle and a lure; there is a spell over her still."

A lure she certainly is, for her monumental ruins are most interesting and, once we have the key to the mystery of her past, most enlightening and inspiring. But her spell of mysterious silence is now over and her puzzle is explained in these pages for the first time and, now that we have shown the way, the task will be taken up and brought to completion by more able men.

So, the generally accepted history of ancient times, such as is found on the shelves of our libraries and taught in our schools, is mostly fiction, made up of fables and myths cleverly composed into history so nicely as to lull all suspicion in the mind of the reader or student as to the fraudulent character of it. Some wonderfully clever writers have been led astray by those deceptions of "history." That this is a fact goes without saying. To make it clear we will give an elucidation of the causes which were back of this gross deception, and the means employed in carrying it out.

CHAPTER III

THE STRUGGLE BETWEEN ROME AND EIRE

THE greatest and most prolonged struggle in ancient times, that we have any account of, or reliable tradition of, was the war between Rome and Ireland, whose name at that time was Eire. We are told by the priests that it was Scotia (from Scoth — choice, select), which is only a mythical name alluding to her Magian Adepts, or Hebrew Priests, of the Sun. It was only after she was sacked and destroyed and her sacred altars laid in ruins by the English invaders at the instigation of Rome that the English priests gave her the name of Ireland (from Ir — the end or "finish"). So, when they finished their foul work of destruction, the English priests of Rome called her Ireland. The Irish Roman Catholic writers tell their people that Ir was one of her old "poetic" names. That is rubbish and false; the above is the truth, and it stands. No more either did Tara, the most sacred place on this earth for thousands of years for the whole Aryan race, have its name changed to "New Grange" just for a whim. It was changed, like so many other Irish names of places, in order that, in the course of time, all memory of its great and important distinction of being the capital of "The Lord of the Isles of the Western Sea," earth's Supreme Pontiff, might be forgotten (see *When the World Will End*, by Rev. Joseph Wild).

Even in far-away India, the island was known as Hiranya, from Eire or Erin, the Isle of the Sun, that is, implying the home of the Sun worship and the Seat of the Great Magian Pontiff, the Sun's chief representative on earth. Ireland is the Great Motherland of the Aryan race and the fictitious and fabled "Atlantis" of Plato. She has suffered too long from the scourge of the invading despoiler. Happily there is a higher and more enlightened sentiment prevailing in Britain today which will bring about a better understanding between the two peoples. It is only when the two nations can meet on equal terms that a friendly and harmonious feeling can be cultivated and exist between them.

It is no part of my purpose to add to troubles that are on the way to be amicably settled, but for the sake of establishing the truth, and without bias, I must explain the part which Britain has taken in the past in destroying and obscuring Ireland's history and also her religious institutions for the profit of Rome. Although England has also profited by the conquest of the island, it has not been all clear gain, and there have been many occasions since when she has repented the help given to Rome. We are glad to note there exists in the world today a growing conscience which taboos piracy and cruel, bloody conquest, along with disregard for the rights of smaller nations.

There have been many seemingly strange upsets in the destiny of nations, one of which is the reversal of position

in the case of England and Ireland. It is a fact, nevertheless, that England is the child or offspring of Ireland
and was a nursling, so to speak, at the breast of this
once great mother, whom she has now persecuted and
oppressed for more than seven hundred years. Let us
hope that a better and brighter day is at hand for both
Eire and England. The peoples of those islands, as
will be shown, are fundamentally of the one Celtic stock.

The great struggle before mentioned, known as the
Punic Wars, are said to have been waged by Rome
against Carthage. This fact is only a partial and misleading statement, meant to deceive and which has
deceived up to this day. Carthage was an Irish colony,
and the name is a mythical one, a compound Irish word,
and alludes to man's besetting sin, sexuality. Philologists have found a striking similarity between Berber and
Irish words even in our own day. The Carthaginian
phase was only a part of the struggle; the wars in Gaul
and Spain were for the same purpose, namely, to destroy
the Irish Church and to set up a universal church and
papacy in Rome through the medium of which Rome
could rule the entire world.

The cause of these wars was said to have been due to
the commercial rivalry between Rome and Carthage.
This was only incidental to the major purpose stated
above. After a struggle lasting for centuries, Rome
finally, with the aid of England, succeeded in destroying
the Irish Church and Papacy, but she has so far fallen
short of ruling the entire world. This ambition of
Rome came to a head and took on new vigor when a

council of the churchmen was called by the Roman
Emperor "Constantine" and assembled at Nice in the
year 325 of our era, known in history as the Council of
Nice. Those men knew what The Great Pyramid
represented and what it was associated with, and our
belief is that it was their purpose to destroy it as they
did so many of the great temples and monuments of the
earlier church. They did not want to leave standing so
much visible evidence of the existence of the former
religious institution which they were going to displace
with a new one of their own making. So, in every age
since, the leaders of the Roman Church have had a conscious knowledge of the part played by their organization
in the suppression of all knowledge concerning the history
of The Great Pyramid, the purpose for which it was built
and who the builders were.

Those astute political priests knew that silence on such
matters was the most efficacious way to have them forgotten, and by absorbing the older church and papacy, in
a few generations there would be none left among the
people who would know anything about such matters.
Therefore, the clerical writers have left us an account
that is full of falsehood and invention, such as the
invasion of the "Vandals" in Europe, in order to account
for the destruction of churches and monasteries as well
as the property of the outraged inhabitants who resisted
despoliation and violence at the hands of the church
forces. We believe that this destruction was carried
out by the organized "Vandals" of the new church,
worked up into a state of fanatical zeal by the clergy;

and what property of the old church they spared was taken over and appropriated, the temples being given new names by the usurpers and used as churches.

Through this campaign of destruction and silence, bolstered up by a false history, Rome figured that none would ever know of the part she played in the undermining of the great Irish Church or the Religion of Iesa. Iesa was the Irish symbolical savior, crucified on the cross, and from him Rome got her Savior "Jesu," substituting the letter *j* for *i*. It is translated into the English language as Jesus.

It was the worship of Iesa, more than any other religion, that prevailed among the people of Europe at the time the Church of Rome began her mission to plunge the world into ignorance and darkness in order that mankind might forget all of the past. Her intention, no doubt, was to destroy all evidence (and she thought she had succeeded well in doing so) by which men in future ages might be able to refute the false and absurd statements which she has given out regarding the source from which she got her Savior Jesus and her Bible. She appropriated them from the Irish, and, to cover up this fact, committed the most heinous and awful crimes against mankind. They were crimes which involved persecutions, slaughter, and untold suffering, the misery and effects of which have remained with us to this day.

All this was done in order that she could have power and foist upon the world a Savior and a Scripture that was taken bodily from the ancient Irish religion and worship. The so-called "Hebrew" Bible did not come from any people distinctly known in history as the "Hebrews," for there never was such a people.. The name "Hebrew" is derived from Heber (from Ea, fire), an Irish name of the Sun. Melisius is the personified Sun, the father of the Irish race in Irish history, and Heber is his brother. Therefore, he is also a personified attribute of the Sun. So, a Hebrew is a priest of the "Fire" and a disciple of the Sun. It is a secret name for the ancient Irish priests of Iesa. It is one of the names by which the church conspirators have camouflaged the ancient Irish priesthood and, by placing the theater of their history and existence over in Palestine, they have up to this day succeeded in making fools of investigators and scholars.

So, the Christian Bible did not come from India, or from Greece, or from Persia, or from "Palestine," but direct from Ireland and its great master priesthood of Iesa. It has been subjected to many additions and alterations both by Roman and by English churchmen behind closed and locked doors, by men pledged to secrecy regarding the things discussed and the manner in which they were to be interpreted and presented to us. The mind of the general reader has been so thoroughly saturated with false information on this and kindred subjects that this digression is necessary to make clear the motives and the course pursued by the Roman Papacy aided by the hierarchy of Britain, which was a part of the Roman Church, to make the substitution of the Irish Savior Iesa and the Bible possible.

In furtherance of that object, it may be said that to

the Church of Rome, more than all else, can be ascribed
the national misfortunes of the Irish race; and, owing
to lack of knowledge of the true cause of their downfall,
the latter day children of the Geal (fair, white, bright —
the Sun), through the influence and organization of the
priests, unwittingly are supporting the institution that
dealt Ireland her death blow. Rome was her impla-
cable enemy for centuries. She was her nemesis. She
raised up enemies against Ireland wherever she could.
In the beginning of a later period of history, England
was the handmaid of the Roman Church, but in more
recent times the relationship became reversed, and Rome,
instead of being the open and avowed enemy, acted as
the secret and insidious auxiliary of England in suppressing the aspirations of the Irish people towards
realizing the national consciousness for self-government
and independence, which was never extinguished in
the hearts of the people. The leaders of the Roman
as well as those of the English High Church are yet
conscious that the star "Leviticus" still sheds its spiritual influence over the "Sacred Isle," and that it is the
homeland of the Bible, and that from the "Select" of
that people were the "Levites." (From Lamh, a hand,
signifying the artificer, the disciple or priest of the Sun.
Hence the symbolic "Lamh Dearg," pronounced lav-
darg, the Red Hand of Ulster. This was a spiritual
symbol and was used as an insignia of the house of
Tyrone.) It has never been compatible with the interests of the Roman Papacy to act otherwise in our
day than as a secret enemy, considering the part which

it had taken in aiding Britain in destroying first the independence of the Irish Nation as a political and commercial power, and second in her suppression and absorption of the National Irish Church, which, up to that time, the year 1169 of our era, had never before been under the sway of Rome but was of itself the greatest church in the world, independent, and once the great Mother Church of all who worshiped the True and Living God.

Up to the middle of the first century of our era, it was the most widespread church in all Europe and the western world. The conquest and absorption of this great church was the constant aim and ambition of the Roman Emperors. Under the lead of the Papacy, it required centuries to bring it about.

It was for this purpose that England was invaded by the Roman arms, in order to strike a vital blow at Ireland which was the seat of power in those islands. England and Scotland had known no other rule up to this time. The Irish Pope and King was the sovereign lord who ruled from his Capital at Tara, and his rule never had been supplanted or displaced in those islands up to this event. It is amusing to see what lapses of memory and what omissions the English and Romanist writers and chroniclers have had and displayed in trying to dodge this most transparent and unacknowledged fact. In order to avoid mentioning it, they have to gloss it over and ignore it, or throw a hazy and uncertain atmosphere about this part of the early history of Britain. There is one very plain fact which stands out before the

student and investigator, and that is that Ireland was
the homeland of the Scotic race; that it was from there
that those islands were ruled; and that it was this power
that Rome had to contend with when she invaded
Britain.

This fact is omitted by the English church writers
because to mention it would need explanations and
might show the reason for the Roman invasion. With
an amazing inconsistency they endeavor to show that
the Irish made their initial conquests in Britain as late
as about the year 240 A.D. Of course, this is plainly
not so, for at this time the Irish power is on the decline.
At this period, the Irish are not making any new conquests, but striving to hold on to what they have always
been in possession of against the Roman invaders.

We find them occupying not only the south and west
parts of Britain but also the east and Cornwall. And
what there were of the Scots (Irish) there at this time
was a people converted into the status of a garrison,
mostly on the defensive in the east of Britain and in
Cornwall. In the west and north as well as in the
southwest they were unconquered. So, instead of this
being the beginning of the Scotic power in Britain, as
they would have us believe, it was the declining period.
They were approaching the end of their long reign in
that country, which was ended in the west and north
of Britain only long after the invasion of the Jutes and
Saxons. Even these barbarians, in time, yielded to
Irish culture, which still remained the greatest intellectual leaven in the island, and became civilized. Brilliant

Irish monks and scholars kept this culture alive, and during the 8th, 9th, and 10th centuries many of them were engaged as teachers and instructors in the establishments of Saxon princes in Britain. This was a growing cause of alarm at Rome.

So, the Irish were the original people of those islands. These are the facts which seem to escape British writers, but, somehow, they find no difficulty in inventing fables to bolster up any supposition which they wish to advance and to give it the color of history.

Rome brought the war to Britain because it was territory which was occupied and ruled over by the Irish Pope-King, and it was to crush this church power that his territory of Britain was invaded. To obtain the coveted prize of the Popedom which was held by the Irish rulers was the great ambition which the Emperors or heads of the Roman State-Church sought to accomplish. There is no doubt whatever but that it was for the purpose of bringing this about that the Danes and the Norwegians were induced to make raids upon and attack the Scots, both in Ireland and Scotland and in the islands of the surrounding seas. Later they raided both Roman and Celt alike as the motive was either plunder or conquest.

We are satisfied that Rome did not stop at employing any means she could find to carry out her ends. By their character "ye shall know them." We find the Danes and Northmen attacking Ireland in the first half of the 9th century and, no doubt, they did effect establishments in some of the seaports like Dublin and

Waterford. Although they came as foes, in time many of them became assimilated with the Irish population. But the constant urge of Rome kept bringing them on from time to time. For the next one hundred years fresh hordes of Vikings came until their final defeat at Clontarf in the year 1014 A.D. In the years 991 to 994 we find Olaf Tryggvasson in England. We are told that he was there converted to Christianity, or, in other words, he became an avowed partisan of Rome. We immediately again find him in Ireland at war with the Irish. He left Dublin to become King of Norway in 995 A.D., and, to make good his espousal of the Roman cause, he forced his people by the terror of the sword to embrace Romanism, or the so-called Christianity.

A writer, evidently a churchman, in the *Encyclopædia Britannica* * (p. 556, Art. "Norway") in an apologetical vein says of this exemplifier of Roman methods of proselyting, "He had been baptized some time during his English expedition, and had taken up Christianity in a more serious manner than was generally the case with the northern converts of his class who as a rule submitted to baptism as a convenient or necessary transaction. Olaf's Christianity does not appear to have been of a very deep or enlightened type, but he was thoroughly in earnest about it, and set himself to enforce its supremacy with the whole energy of his character.

"And, in an incredibly short time, if he had not exactly succeeded in making his subjects Christian, he had at least made it very unsafe for them to be anything else.

* Ninth Edition.

By force, or gifts, by persuasion, or even by torture
if necessary — for his anger was sometimes cruel enough
— he soon scarcely left a man of note unbaptized in
Norway."

Now, I should say that this Olaf was a very apt con-
vert, and that he imbibed the spirit of Roman Christianity according to example and precedent. He evidently understood the meaning of his own mission to
Ireland as an ally of Rome, and he surely took his baptism and his lesson well, despite the "faint praise" of
this cleric, who seems on the whole pleased with the
work he accomplished. Any bishop would be. He
says further: "Perhaps the strangest thing is not merely
that he attained his end so rapidly, but that he did so
without rousing and alienating the people. His splendid
personal appearance, his wonderful strength and skill
in arms, his inexhaustible courage and energy, and the
frank, chivalrous nature, bright and joyous when in
quiet, but capable of terrible passion when enraged —
seem to have attracted everyone at the time."

This writer stresses exceedingly in trying to portray
this fiend and ruffian in qualities which might make
him acceptable to anyone worthy to be called human.
There was a very good and sufficient reason why the
people were "attracted" to him, because they were in his
power. We read of him in *Bible Myths* (T. W.
Doane, p. 449): "Even among the Norwegians, the
Christian sword was unsheathed. They clung tena-
ciously to the worship of their forefathers, and numbers
of them died real martyrs for their faith, after suffering

the most cruel torments from their persecutors. It was by sheer compulsion that the Norwegians embraced Christianity. The reign of Olaf Tryggvasson, a Christian King of Norway, was in fact entirely devoted to the propagation of the new faith, by means most revolting to humanity. His general practice was to enter a district at the head of a formidable force, summon a Thing (an assembly or congress of the freemen), and give the people the alternative of fighting with him or of being baptized. Most of them, of course, preferred baptism to the risk of a battle with an adversary so well prepared for combat, and the recusants were tortured to death with fiendlike ferocity and their estates confiscated."

This explains why the people were not "alienated" from this Roman apostle, despite the apology of his clerical admirer and eulogist. Thus is shown the purpose and the object of Norse and Danish incursions into Ireland. Priestly fictions and inventions have had their day, and it would be too bad indeed if such silly falsehoods as have heretofore been accepted should forever, as they were intended and expected to do, prevent mankind from getting a true and clear insight into the motives which were back of those invasions and which led up to those historic occurrences. The motives are, as shown, most obvious, and enlightened men will accept and acknowledge them.

These writers serve up a myth as history which contains an idea cloaked or hidden for the express purpose of deceiving the people as a whole. Here is an example.

It is from English history, as written by the priests, and shows the way in which they have blinded the people and kept the truth under cover for ·their own benefit. In English history we are told that after the Roman forces were withdrawn from Britain, the country was overrun by the Scots and Picts and that a British prince or duke by the name of Vortigern invited the German tribes to come in and take possession of the country. The Angles, Saxons, and Jutes came under the leadership of the two brothers, Hengest and Horsa. We are told that warfare ensued for about forty years. Of the two brothers Horsa was killed in a battle with Vortigern. After this happens, Hengest and his son Aesc seized the royal purple and became kings. A writer of the history topic "England" in the *Encyclopædia Britannica* (9th Ed., p. 269) very naïvely says: "In all this there is nothing like romance. It is a matter-of-fact kind of history, which might be preserved by a runic chronicle, which might almost be preserved by tradition." It is not quite so straightforward and simple a tale as he would have us believe, and it was not meant to be, as we will show in what follows.

"Vortigern" is a Celtic or Irish word with the first syllable inflected. It is an alteration of the word *Morthiarna*. The *t* is silent and *M* is inflected, as is common in the Celtic, and is given the sound of *V*. The word is phonetically pronounced Vor-agee-ern, and signifies a great lord, a prince or ruler. The forty years, in which the warfare is said to go on, is the "sacred number" forty, the term of years in each incarnation

or life in which a "religious" man is theoretically in a
battle with himself to overcome his lower nature, his
passions and desires. Hengest is formulated from the
Celtic word Ong, a name of the Sun, and personified
as it is here it signifies a Worshiper of the Sun, a leader,
a Bishop.

In ancient Irish mythical lore, the Sun is said to have
a charioteer, or horseman. The Celtic word for horse is
"eac," hence Eactoir, the valiant man of deeds, anglicized as Hector. In this myth he is presented to us very
nicely disguised in English dress, so that you do not quite
recognize him, as Horsa (also a Priest of the Sun) who
is also a leader and a Bishop. Aesc is an abbreviation
of the Irish word Easboc. It is the name of an order
or degree of the ancient Irish priesthood of Iesa, and
it is the name word for "Bishop." So, we are informed,
under a heavy layer of covering, that "Aesc" was a
Bishop also and a spiritual leader of the invading horde
to rob and slay the people of Britain in order to enable
the Roman Church to maintain the foothold it had
secured and was about to lose.

In the covert language of the myth, the High Priest,
Heirophant or Demigod, is always a prince, duke, lord,
or nobleman. The facts of this bit of mythical history,
to state it in open manner, is that the head of the Roman
Church in Britain, carrying out the instructions of his
master in Rome, instigated the two German tribes to
invade England under the leadership of their two bishops,
of whom "Horsa" was slain in battle and "Hengest"
and "Aesc," the successor of Horsa, more fortunately

survived. In time they grasped royal power and became kings.

The truth about the invasion is that there were only two German tribes (as such) engaged in it, though there is no doubt but that there were many adventurers encouraged to join with them in the undertaking through the persuasion of Roman emissary priests.

These two tribes were. the Jutes and Saxons. The so-called tribe of "Angles" is a fiction invented by Anglophile writers of a later day. It is part of a plot to obscure the Celtic or Gaelic element, which is the greatest in the composition of the English race, and to unduly emphasize the German element, which is comparatively small and almost non-existent today with the exception of some of the nobility and the reigning family.

This bias was very pronounced during the reign of Queen Victoria. The fact that her consort was a German prince gave added impetus to propaganda which had already been long in force to suppress or belittle everything of Celtic cultural nature. So it became popular to claim that whatever was of excellence in English life was due to the German element in the race. This false impression was helped to become fixed in the popular mind by just such invention of spurious history and by giving out false accounts regarding events of the past, such as the story of the "Angles" being a German tribe. The false impression was purposely made upon the mind of the English people that the term "Anglo-Saxon" meant that they were a race of German descent.

This is a delusion which has been diligently fostered. The propagation of this fiction came to a sudden stop when the World War began, but, since the war, the same propaganda, the same systematic falsehood and misrepresentation, has been in evidence. It has found a voice through our American press. I took the matter up in a letter, the salient points of which I here give, which I sent to a leading newspaper. The letter was published under the caption, "Says English are Celtic in Blood as well as in Speech." This statement was apparently so radically at variance with the claims of the propagandists that it might well be expected to bring forth a reply or that an attempt at contradiction would be made if possible. No reply came because the propagandists might well have considered that it was a dangerous subject and the more discussion it received, the greater would be the exposure of the false history which has been so extensively written and circulated.

The letter, in part, is as follows:

Sir:

In a recent issue I read the statement that "Celtic hardly exists in the English language and still less in the English blood." I wish to refute this statement. It is absolutely false. The basis of the English speech is undeniably Celtic and it cannot very well be eradicated without destroying the English language. Any person laying the least claim to scholarship should know that fact. The above-quoted statement savors very much of the fashion in vogue with

English writers of the Victorian era to eschew everything Celtic and claim affinity with the "German Cousin." But the rough handling the British troops received at the battle of Mons, and subsequently, opened the eyes of the English people to the true fact that Celtic blood was the basis of the English race. Now that the war is over, the same evil tactics of division and dissension are being employed to keep the English and the Irish peoples apart by means of hatred and animosity, as if there were nothing of kinship between them of old. The common people of Ireland and England never had a quarrel with one another. Dean Swift, a Protestant, of Dublin, tried to get the Irish people to compose their differences by citing a case such as this to them : Why should men quarrel because one wanted his eggs boiled soft and the other wanted his boiled hard? No real cause for a quarrel. I am glad to see the growing union of political sentiment between the Irish representatives and the Labor Party of England which represents the democratic and progressive elements of the English people. I feel that they are, for the best good of all, determined .to give justice to Ireland in order that friendship and mutual confidence may exist where formerly hatred and mistrust prevailed. I would advise our English, Irish, and Scottish brothers to look askance at anybody who would try to sow seeds of dissension among them. . . .

Now, as to whether there is any Celtic in the English language, let me cite just a few well beloved words of common everyday English speech. We will take first the English word "all." Its root derivation is Celtic and means "universal, great, mighty, a race, a generation, all." Next take "altitude." The root of this word is the Celtic word "alt," meaning a high place or eminence. Then the English word "river." The root of it is the Celtic word "ri," meaning to run, ria — running. Hence our name for a brook — a run. Another Celtic name for river is "Amhan," pronounced "Ahwin"; hence, by corruption of English pronunciation, we have Stratford-on-Avon, that is, Stratford-on-river, Shakespeare's home. Then take "London." The name is Celtic and is a compound of two Celtic words, "Lann" — strong, and "dun" — a fort or city. Hence, London, Strong City. Next the English word "lion," a word dear to every Englishman. The root of it is the Celtic word "leo," meaning a limb, member, strength; hence, lion (Lat. "leo" is derived from the same source, as Latin is a daughter of the Celtic). The word "rose" is taken from the Celtic word "ros," meaning bright, shining, pleasant, agreeable. The word "red," the color of the English flag, is taken from the Celtic "ru" or "rot" (the Germans also got the word from the same source). Then we come to the Englishman's soubriquet, "John Bull." It is surely a Celtic word. It means the fructifier, the male principle. The Celtic word is "Bel." The Scottish call it "Bil" and the English "Bull." Now, dear sir, while the impulse is still strong to proceed

further, I think that I have advanced enough of
evidence to show the great Celtic foundation of
English speech, that it is rooted in the Celtic mother
tongue. It is the same with English blood — it is
mostly Celtic; and while it is not my purpose to go
into this at length, I will briefly say that, while the
English people were at different times inoculated with
a strain of other blood, it has long since been eliminated, for it is the same with a race as it is with the
earth itself. It reverts back to first principles.
"The tail cannot wag the dog."

The English people have been able to assimilate
every strain which has come among them; hence their
virility. I will conclude in the words of Shakespeare,
"There are stranger things in this world, Horatio,
than you or I wot of."

What is now called England was from time immemorial occupied by the Celtic or Gaelic race. In the
Gaelic tongue the name of the race is Angaoidhil, pronounced with the *d* silent, Angael, signifying the Gael.
This country, then, as a most natural consequence of
the name of the race which occupied it was known to the
Germans as Angaoidhil-land, or the country of the
Gaels. The name has persisted and has never been
changed except in so far as the corruption of English
pronunciation has made the slight change phonetically
from Angael-land to Angle-land, and finally to its
modern form, England. The name is truly derived from
its ancient race, the Gaels, in a most obvious and natural

manner. So the term "Anglo-Saxon," which a few
have so ardently cultivated, has unwittingly served but
to perpetuate the memory of Angael-land's ancient
people, while the covert purpose was to suppress all
knowledge of this important fact. The fiction of the
story of the Angles as being one of the invading tribes
may be easily understood also by the fact that, in the
cryptic account given of the invasion, an account written
by the priests, there were only two leaders or bishops
mentioned — Hengest and Horsa — "one for each tribe."
If there had been three tribes instead of two, there
would have been three bishops at their head to lead
them. For it was always the "Bishop" who assumed
power and leadership. This fact is shown in the narrative that, on the death of Bishop "Horsa," his successor, Bishop "Aesc," and Bishop "Hengest" grasped
royal power and became kings. Aesc is called the son
of Hengest only in a religious sense, as he was "created"
or made bishop by the latter and, hence, is his "son."

This illustrates how little dependence can be placed
on some of the history that has come down to us from the
priests. It is most unreliable, and a great deal of it is
pure falsehood and fable, especially that which has
come to us from English and Roman writers.

So we see the work of Rome in the Jute and Saxon
invasion of England always pursuing the same object —
the conquest and acquisition of the Irish Church. No
one needs to entertain a doubt about this fact. Later
on when disputes arose in England, between the Church
and King, we find Pope Hildebrand urging William

of Normandy to overthrow the English king and in that way to strengthen his own power in that quarter a thing very necessary to Rome. The result proved it so later, in the reign of Henry II of England, who aided Rome to reach her long-sought goal. the conquest of Ireland and the suppression and absorption of the Irish National Church of Iesa, its institutions. Savior and Bible.

Although Rome had grown great in power by the time that she invaded Britain, she still had a difficult struggle ahead of her. She found that the closer she came to Ireland, where the Irish were near their base of supplies the more stubborn became the opposition. After a period of occupancy of four hundred years or so the invasion of England failed to bring Ireland and the Irish Church under her power.

At about the latter part of the fourth century. disintegration within and invasion from without forced her to cease for the time her warfare on the Irish (Scots and Picts, who are the same race, from the north and caused Rome to withdraw her forces from Britain never to return as an armed state power. But the Roman Church had in that period become established in England. It got a firm foothold in the occupied territory. It had not yet spread to Wales or Scotland But she had accomplished one part of her mission to destroy the Irish Church and thereby enable herself to set up a universal papacy in Rome. It remained for time and circumstance to enable her to accomplish the former; the latter ambition has never been fully realized.

While the Irish nation was confronted with the menace
of invasion and conquest by Roman armies, it remained
united and invincible against the mightiest power on
earth. Although the ranks of the population must have
been pretty well depleted of material for military service, after centuries of warfare, they succeeded in preserving their political and spiritual independence.
They survived, perhaps, the longest period of continued
military strain which any people of like numbers were
ever subjected to.

But with the removal of the menace of Roman invasion, reaction set in and the relaxation from the
necessities and rigors incident to constant war gave the
people opportunity to apply themselves to the occupa-
tions of a peaceful life and to cultivate the arts and
sciences which had been neglected and many of which
had no doubt been forgotten. They also cultivated
the spiritual life, which was in abeyance during the centuries of warfare. In the succeeding centuries, Ireland
became again as in former ages the center of learning
and the home of the sciences, which she was in the beginning before the first migration of the Irish or Aryan
race towards the East, or the Rising Sun, for they were
truly the "Children of Light and Knowledge."

After the withdrawal of the Roman forces from
Britain, it was the purpose of the Irish Pope-King,
through the medium of the monastic orders, to spread
knowledge and science throughout all the countries of
Europe. But this was in direct conflict with the policy
of Rome, which was to spread ignorance and darkness.

She did not want the history of the past to be known. It would interfere with her purpose and defeat it.

The Irish Church hoped to regain some of the lost ground after the withdrawal of the Roman armies from Britain and eventually would have done so, had not Rome succeeded in raising up new enemies against her. In the German tribes of the Jutes and Saxons she found willing allies. They were won over by Rome to invade England, as the spoils were enticing. Irish missionaries went again to the continent and endeavored to spread the light. John Dunn, Scotus (the Irish were called Scots), founded a monastery and school at Ratisbon on the Danube. Many went to other places, but all to no purpose, as the opposition of Rome was too strong to overcome. The loot of the Irish Church was yet to be obtained. Later, we are told, some of them were received at the court of Charlemagne, for the Irish Pope was still "the Lord of the Isles of the Western Sea." But the alluring inducements offered by Rome appealed more to Charlemagne's cupidity and ambition for power. And Charlemagne being a politician went with Rome and became Emperor. He then embarked on a war of religious conquest with the sword against the Germans in order to force them to bow to the Roman Church yoke and relinquish their adherence to the Celtic Church. This practically put an end to any chance of success for the mission of the Irish monks on the continent. All who now wished for education and the higher learning had to go to Ireland for it, and thither they went by the thousands and were welcomed.

They were domiciled and given both food and tuition free. This continued from the period shortly following the withdrawal of the Roman forces from England until the coming of the Danes and Northmen to Ireland.

It was during this period of the revival of learning that the Irish masters are said to have laid the foundation of our modern university system, of which such great schools as Harvard, Yale, Columbia, Dartmouth, Cornell, and others are part. Let us give credit where credit is due. This was not the beginning, but only the renaissance of Irish learning on the continent of Europe, as British writers would have us believe. This is on a par with their juggling of fact regarding the occupancy and rule of Britain by the Irish Pope-Kings previous to the Roman invasion.

The Irish Magian Priesthood had always had this great learning. It was handed down through a secret cult of adepts from time immemorial. It was this which enabled them to erect the immense and perfectly proportioned Great Pyramid of Iesa. It should not be any surprise to us that learning fell into a state of decline during the great struggle with Rome. It could not very well be cultivated under such conditions, yet however much diminished, it was never extinguished. Had Ireland been a part of the Continent of Europe, instead of being an island, it might have been different and this revival could not have taken place. We are all living witnesses of the great inroads which were made in the ranks of the undergraduates in our own colleges during one year and a half of warfare in the late World War. We may well ponder on what the conditions would have been if the war had continued for ten or twenty years, to say nothing of several centuries of warfare. We all felt keenly the shortages in supplies and the scarcity of many articles of use, in which manufacture ceased owing to the fact that the nation's energy and man power was being directed to the manufacture and production of the things that were used solely for the prosecution of the war. If this continued for a great length of time, we can easily see where many of the arts and sciences, in fact culture in general, would have been neglected and as a natural result forgotten.

When we think what a comparatively small nation Ireland was in those days beside mighty Rome, we may well think it a miracle that learning did not perish from the island altogether. It is to this island we must look for the original source from which our learning and science came. Here is where it was first conceived, nurtured, and cultivated, and from here it spread throughout the entire world. Her sacred literature has been pilfered by Rome and her learning and mythology handed over and accredited to Greece by these same English Romanist tricksters. In the mythology which they have stolen and handed over to Greece, they have covered up and secretly preserved, for their own knowledge, the very source from which it came, for, as the Greeks said, they "knew not where their traditions came from, for they were strange to them." Of course, they were strange and are so yet, except to the knowing ones. The names of the gods and goddesses have been changed to some extent to suit the purpose of the deception. For instance, Anna is the mother of the Irish Gods, and we find her accredited to the Greeks with her temple at Ephesus, her statue that of a female figure crowned and with many breasts to suckle her children. She is presented as conceived and personified by the Irish priest philosophers as the many-breasted "Mother" of the gods. She is the female principle of Deity, the Great Mother which sustains all life. They made her over as Diana (God Anna) and Rome has stolen her and translated her into "Saint Ann," the mother of Mary (from the Irish Muire, the Sea), and the grandmother of Iesus (Jesus). It is irrefutable.

They have taken the Irish Hercules (the personified Sun, from Her, meaning above, and Cu, meaning wolfhound or swift, the "High Swift One") and made him into Heracles. Under the guise of the myth, when this god goes to Ireland and places himself on Mount Abas (Ab, a father or pope) and kills Geryon (an Irish name of the Sun and always connected with the Sun worship, the Irish Pope and Father, Representative of the Sun and the Head of His worshipers on earth), he steals cattle and brings them to Italy. Do we not here find a hidden allusion to the fact that the new "Heracles" took possession of the Irish papacy and the rest of the plunder he brought to Italy as "cattle"? The myth states that "Hercules went to Erytheia, an island somewhere in the remote West, beyond the pillars of Hercules, where was a giant named Geryon (Irish Grian, the glowing aspect). When Hercules reached the island, he placed himself on Mount Abas. Geryon has cattle which at night he keeps in a dark cave in the remote West. Hercules slays Geryon and ships the cattle into the vessel of the Sun, and, landing them safely, drives them through Iberia, Gaul, and across the Alps into Italy" (Murray's *Manual of Mythology*, pp. 292–3).

Those writers do not mention the fact that Eire was the island in the West and the Home of Sun worship referred to in the myth. "Erytheia" is but a name for Eire, under camouflaged spelling. The root of the word is Iar, the West, the Western Isle, behind which the Sun sets.

The Goddess Ceres is also Irish and means the Earth. There is no letter *K* in the Celtic alphabet and *C* has the sound of the English *K*. The word in Irish is pronounced Keres, while in English it has the soft sound as Ceres. This difference in spelling and sound has been taken advantage of and utilized in carrying out the deception. We declare without fear of successful contradiction that Ireland is the homeland of these myths and the island alluded to in the West.

Even "Olympus," the seat of the Greek Gods, is a compound Irish name with a Greek ending. It is formed by combining the words Ollam, a doctor or professor of science, and Fis, wisdom; hence, Mount Olympus, the Mount of Wisdom and the seat of the Gods. For, of course, the gods are full of wisdom. This seat has been translated to Greece from Ireland. "Seiscean" at Tara was Mount Olympus, or, as the name implies, the "head or seat of Wisdom," the supreme Pope. It never was in Greece. The whole scheme is quite plain and clear when it is pointed out. The wonder is that somebody did not discover it before. Now, as it is all plain, especially to the scholar who can read and translate Irish and recognize its idioms, a new perspective appears before us. (The name Tara implies the Father, and read it the other way and it spells arat, Arhat, a divine man.)

We are led to believe that this deception was well known to Lord Bacon, for he said: "The mythology of the Greeks, which their oldest writers do not pretend to have invented, was no more than a light air, which had passed from a more ancient people into the flutes of the Greeks, which they modulated to such descants as best suited their fancies" (*Atlantis*, p. 283). It is no surprise at all to us that a plot was hatched up against Bacon, and that he was put to death. He gave out too much to be tolerated by unscrupulous and designing persons.

Such candor and plain speaking was quite contrary to the purpose of the English government and hierarchy, and such frankness, if not suppressed, would be fatal to the statecraft and policy of the men who were shaping England's future in that ambitious age. This may have been the cause of his being put to death, for he betrayed state secrets, although malfeasance in office was the charge made against him. However, we still see the successors of those men sitting in the House of Lords as "My Lord Bishop," keeping in close touch with the pulsebeats of the British State.

Ireland has been terribly mistreated through the selfishness of Rome and England. I hope that in this enlightened age, when the spirit of inquiry is abroad in search of truth, that men and women will not let prejudice or preconceived ideas, formed in the absence of fuller knowledge, stand in the way of the acceptance of the truths herein stated though called to their attention for the first time.

It surely is time, in the name of righteousness, that justice be done, and, as far as possible, that the great wrong may be redressed by allowing the great Aryan Mother, metaphorically speaking, to arise to her feet and to set her own house in order.

Scholars and investigators have been very much led astray in the past by accepting as facts Roman and British fiction dressed up in the sober and matter-of-fact garb of History. Those inventors of history would have us direct our attention to any other country than to Ireland. Such complete silence on the part of the arch-conspirators surely did arouse a just suspicion, which upon investigation has yielded such splendid and most convincing proofs of the foulest plot in all human annals.

This plot not only comprehended the pilfering of all of the appurtenances of the Irish Church of Iesa, — the Bible, Savior Iesa (Jesus), property and institutions, literature, etc., — but also the suppression of the Irish language, and, finally, the annihilation or dispersion of the race.

We have been told through Roman and British sources that our learning came from some Asiatic country, perhaps Assyria, Persia, or Arabia, Greece, or Egypt itself. Any one of these countries would serve equally well the purpose of the arch-plotters who came so near to killing off the Irish race that only a small remnant of it was left to survive at one time. They were so reduced in numbers and circumstances that there was no thought in the minds of the English rulers of those days that they would ever again increase in numbers or advance in enlightenment to any extent, or, at least, ever be able to offer any serious resistance to English rule in Ireland.

The priests were employed in writing and concocting a false history, one that would not contain any mention of the nature of her former greatness, or the achievements and discoveries for which the whole civilized world is indebted to her. The very discoveries of the arts and sciences, credit for which discoveries would make any people great, were denied her in the new "Histories," and the credit has been given mainly to Greece with other transfers already mentioned. But we say that it was in Ireland that our civilization arose, and that it was there that the cereals were developed from the grasses. It was on this island that "barley" was first grown, the grain that is particularly associated with the life of an abstemious priesthood. Here we find also the birthplace of Mathematics, Geometry, Navigation, Astronomy, Medicine, Chemistry, and the arts which are commonly called Egyptian. British lexicographers, and others taking their cue from them, in giving the derivation of the word chemistry, refer us to Egyptian, Greek, Latin, or even a Dutch or German root for it; but Cleland (quoted in Webster's Dictionary) derives it from the Celtic root word Kheym* (Chem), fire, which is the true derivation, as fire is the chemical agency in all nature. The Celtic Master Adepts established that science on its true basis. It was in Ireland that the sciences were brought to perfection and the names under which this fact is masked, such as Egyptian, Chaldean, Phoenician, Cushite, Ethiopian, etc., are only names devised by the priests to deceive. This will be shown later on.

Ireland in those days was the mistress of the seas and the great commercial and trading nation of the world. Her vessels and intrepid seamen visited the harbors and ports of every sea where trade and barter was carried on. (See Donnolly's *Atlantis*.) Atlantis is the name under which these plotters have sought to sink Ireland and bury her great past in the oblivion of the bed of the ocean. The name Atlantis was formulated for this very reason and to secretly signify and commemorate her past. The word Atlantis signifies "the illustrious land of wisdom." It is a compound Irish name composed of three words and justifiably applied to Ireland. But it has been done secretly by the British priests of Rome, as one may infer from the fact that they have this Isle of Atlantis lying at the bottom of the Atlantic Ocean. "At" means illustrious, "Lan" means land or church, and "Tis" means wisdom. It is a camouflaged name for the "sacred" island and the great Magian priesthood

---

* Cleland used an English form in spelling the word by using the letter *K*, which is often used instead of the Celtic *C*, there being no *K* in the Irish alphabet. The Irish form of the word is Com or Coem.

which was established there whose ruler was at the head
of all organized religion and the leader of all who worshiped the supreme Deity.

The deception practiced has been successful for a
long time, but it could not last forever. The connection
of the priest and myth at last became apparent and the
solution of the riddle of history was found and the
fiction is exposed.

The people of this island discovered the mariner's
compass and had it in use from remote ages. The story
that the compass came from China or that the Portuguese
obtained it from Mohammedan sailors on the coast of
Africa, is fictitious and is similar to other fictions which
have been put into circulation by either credulous or
very designing persons.

Their voyages to Iceland alone is presumptive evidence
sufficient to establish that fact, for in later times, when
the first Northmen visited that distant island, they
found evidence that Irish monks had been there long
before. Their long voyages across the Atlantic Ocean
to both North and South America is further presumptive
evidence to confirm our belief in this fact. The voyages
of those "Phoenicians" were not haphazard or dependent
on a guess. The communication between Ireland and
both Americas, North and South, was constant and
sustained. The extensive and, for that time, highly
advanced civilization which they established on both
those continents amply warrants this belief. The
remains of their works are in our own country, but much
more so in Mexico, Yucatan, and South America. In-

vestigation and research will prove the truth of these statements. The monuments still remaining in those countries are unmistakable proofs as to who their authors were. The existence of both sphinx and pyramidal remains in Yucatan is not due to mere coincidence or chance.

The art of music was developed by them and cultivated to a greater extent than in any other country. It was truly the homeland of music. The proof of this fact remains yet in evidence, after centuries of more or less neglect, in the fact that, of the thirty-four thousand tunes known in European music, a little more than seventeen thousand are of Irish origin. This fact of itself affords a most wonderful testimony for the psychologist and the thinker of the past accomplishments of this people in the art of music. It is the same with a race as it is with an individual, — it requires time to develop any gift or art. And the fact that they still possess it to such a degree, after such a long period of national decadence and neglect, proves by its being there in such wonderful measure that it is the result of generations of past culture.

CHAPTER IV

THE COMPACT OF ROME AND ENGLAND FOR THE CONQUEST OF IRELAND

WHEN Nicholas Breakspear, an Englishman, was elected Pope of the Roman Church in the year 1154 A.D., he issued a bull granting, without any right whatever, through pure presumption, a permit to King Henry II of England to invade and seize Ireland. The time was at hand for the Roman Church to achieve the second part of her mission to acquire possession of the church of Iesa through the conquest of the Irish nation. Although the Roman Empire had ceased to exist as formerly, its very soul was the Roman Church which continued on with the same ambition, relentlessly pursuing its quarry, the conquest of the Irish Church and all it involved. By this time the power of the church had grown to such an extent that the Roman Pope had assumed to exercise the prerogative of assent and dissent to whatever activities kings or princes might venture to engage in, all the more so as the church was firmly established in the countries of western Europe. But the Papacy of the *original church* of the One True God was yet to be crushed and its light extinguished before the Roman aspirant could plume himself as the supreme Pope. King Henry, on his part, for justification in the eyes of the world and to appear to act on worthy authority with warranted right to enter upon a campaign of murder and spoliation against a friendly nation which had been guilty of no offense against his kingdom, proceeded to act on the Pope's permit and embark on the conquest. The church, on its part, was not dilatory in setting in motion the means for the consummation of its long-cherished ambition.

For this purpose an English Pope was chosen by the Consistory at Rome, in order that an English King could be enlisted through him to undertake to do this work for the Roman Church. It was necessary to enlist one as little troubled with conscience as the Pope himself and who could raise the necessary force to make the murderous venture a success. So Pope Adrian IV, for this was the title he took when he had a "new name given" to him by Rome, urged Henry to invade Ireland. The king was to be rewarded with the plunder which he was to obtain from that rich and fertile country besides the annual tax to be levied and the fees to be collected for the crown thereafter.

Adventurer though Henry was, and perhaps eager for the expedition, he saw fit, before launching such a campaign of violence against a neighboring people who were at peace with his countrymen, to cover up under the "permit" of this usurping Pope his evil designs. The project was later approved by Pope Alexander III with consistent moral turpitude. It was stipulated in the agreement between Henry and the Pope that the king would cause to be collected the sum of one penny from each house on the island to be forwarded to enrich the

coffers of the church and to recompense it for the moral
and spiritual countenance it gave to the initial step of a
crime which was to lead in time to almost complete destruction of the Irish race, under the English Government's policy of "to hell or to Connaught" with the Irish
people.   This policy almost decimated the Irish race and
also brought about a most determined effort on the part
of the government and clergy to keep the English people
systematically deceived and falsely instructed as to the
real cause of the outrages and massacres committed in
Ireland by the English forces.   The English clergy dared
not tell them that they were begun to cover up and hide
the true source of Christianity, the Bible and the Savior
"Jesus" and the Papacy.   The people were made to see
only the obvious cause, the resistance of the Irish people
to being dispossessed of their lands for the benefit of the
English and later the Scotch settlers to whom they had
been given.

The province of Connaught was rocky and had a
poorer soil than the other provinces of the country, and
what good land there was in the province was given to
the English settlers and government adherents. Con-
sequently, it could maintain only a small remnant of the
people.   Thousands of them died from hardships due to
exposure to the inclemencies of the weather and to
diseases caused by poor and insufficient food, while the
Roman Pope and his staff of Cardinals sang hosannahs
in grand display before the Roman people and in secret
behind their backs plotted murder and the degradation
of a great nation.

In order that some idea may be had of the ferocity and severity of the wars waged in Ireland due to the Romish-British plot and invasion, I shall quote from a writer who is before all an apologist for Rome and Britain (*Encyclopædia Britannica*, 9th Edition, Vol. 13, pp. 264-5, Article "Ireland"). This writer says in regard to the constant warfare carried on there, especially of the war of Elizabeth under Ormond against the Geraldines in Munster: "The horrors of this war it is impossible to exaggerate. The Four Masters say that the lowing of a cow or the voice of a plowman could scarcely be heard from Cashel to the farthest point in Kerry." At this point in his narrative he attempts to minimize the effect of his previous statement of rapine and horrors, and would cast a doubt over it by saying that "Ormond, who, with all his severity, was honorably distinguished by good faith, claimed to have killed five thousand men in a few months." One does not have to be very keen to see his idea in clothing Ormond with such honor and truthfulness. It is to create an impression in the mind of the reader that, after a war of "a few months," an indefinite period, such a small number of killed would not bespeak very great horror or severity. I am not much impressed with his "honor" or the truthfulness of the man Ormond, or with the statement attributed to him, as a commander; but, if he personally slew that number of men, they must have been unarmed and defenseless, and such a deed in itself would destroy every vestige of the attribute of honor from his character and stamp him as a veritable ruffian. And it is safe to say that, if he had not possessed

ruffianly qualities, he would not be Elizabeth's choice
for that mission of destruction; for she herself was dishonest, as this writer apologetically admits, by saying
that she was surrounded by enemies and that many of
her predecessors were as crooked as she, and less upright
in intention (p. 265).

In fact, when the truth is told, the British element
which engaged in the conquest of Ireland was, with their
successors for hundreds of years, as coarse, as low, and as
brutal men as could be found. This writer before quoted
shows (p. 261, Vol. 13, *Enc. Brit.*) that when fortune
did not always favor them in Ireland during the reign of
Henry V, half of the English colony fled to England and
were found to be so vicious a lot that the people of England could not endure them and they had to be ordered
out of the country. Many of them, by offers of high pay,
were induced to enlist in Henry's army for service in
France. He further admits the brutality of those wars
by saying that "the Irish wars had not been a good
school of humanity."

The fact is that the English policy, from the beginning,
in Ireland was not a humane one. Of the Ormond
cruelties before cited, the same witness, who quotes
Edmund Spenser, says that "famine slew far more than
the sword." He further says that "the survivors were
unable to walk but crawled out of the woods and glens."
It may well be surmised that when an army of cut-
throats bent on annihilation falls upon a rural population,
there could not be many who could find secure shelter in
the woods or glens.

Spenser says of those who came forth, "They looked like anatomies of death; they did eat the dead carrion and one another soon after, insomuch as the very carcasses they spared not to scrape out of the graves; and to a plot of water-cresses or shamrocks they flocked as to a feast."

The section of the country which was ravaged and laid bare might easily have had at that time a population of 200,000 souls. History records that Oliver Cromwell ravaged that same district seventy years later and left it so bare that he was reported as saying that, if a crow ate while flying over it, he would have to bring his food with him. After the Cromwellian massacres the population of the island was at a low ebb, said to have been 850,000 only. It is a safe estimate to say that in former times the population was from eight to ten millions, if not more; for it was a religious axiom with the people — "Be ye fruitful and multiply."

One of the adjuncts considered necessary by the British hierarchy, acting for Rome, to make Henry's expedition a success, and to build up a false history which would serve the interests of the Church and the English Government for future generations, was a "publicity bureau." It was established to assist in carrying out the papal policy, not only of destroying the Irish Church and Nation, but also to put into effect a well-thought-out plan. It was worthy of the original bishop, whom Machiavelli had in mind for his diplomatic model, to vilify them before all mankind and posterity. Rome had then, as she has today, in her ranks, men of all grades of conscience and versatility, some of whom she could always find fit to carry out her ends, however vile they might be. The "old man of the mountain" had his faithful adherents and his emissaries likewise. A priest known in history as Geraldus Cambrensis was duly appointed to do this dastardly work, and it is mainly due to the false and slanderous writings and fictitious alibis set up in his "Vaticinal" history and in his work entitled "The Conquest of Ireland" that a documentary foundation of history, composed of willful and vicious falsehoods, was laid down, and British writers have ever since made use of it.

Geraldus's fables are supported, as it was arranged that they should be, by another "set up," who is called Jocelyn. Thus did this knavish priest furnish a false documentary history of Ireland from which both material and ideas have since been taken to traduce her. And especially during this last century were they industriously circulated abroad through British propaganda. That his slanders are discredited today is not the fault of his sponsors, but it shows the base vileness and dishonesty of the Roman and British propagandists. A British clerical writer in the *Encyclopædia Britannica** (Art. Ireland) frankly admits that "in spite of the enormities and filthinesses which Geraldus says defiled the Irish Church, nothing worse could be found than marriages within the prohibited degrees, and trifling irregularities about Baptism." So it becomes very clear that the invasion of Ireland by Henry II was a plot instigated by

* 9th Edition.

the Roman Church; for, if she had been established in Ireland before that event, her discipline alone would have been enough to correct any such "trifling" abuses if any such existed.   To correct such trifling abuses would not be a cause for a war involving an invasion of the country, incited by a church whose mission is professedly "peace on earth, good will toward men."   It is one of the most glaring and barefaced falsehoods ever invented, and they expected too much when they supposed that a fiction which was believed in an ignorant age would also continue to be believed in an enlightened one.

The Irish Nation was made the victim of a foul conspiracy of the Roman Church and England.   She has been most terribly crucified between two thieves, and it is time for the best element among the English people to correct this great wrong.   By such falsehoods, British priests and writers have endeavored to cast discredit upon Ireland's history in order to minimize any interest which might otherwise be shown by students of research, and so that no investigation or research could be made which might lead to damaging discoveries.   Besides, it was intended to dampen and discourage any interest which the Irish might arouse in foreign countries toward winning moral or material aid in realizing their national independence.

It is mainly from British sources that people in general, even in so-called enlightened countries, have gleaned their very limited knowledge of the Irish people or of their history, and formed their impressions based on meager and distorted information.   The British press is most devotedly engaged in the same effort in our own day, and, according to published information, quite a few of the publishers of our own country have been subsidized to misrepresent things Irish, while the British Government has allowed its trained forces to commit barbarities against unoffending citizens in Ireland. But the people of Irish race, wherever they have cast their lot, by their capacity and wonderful achievements in all lands, have demonstrated the falsity of those slanders.

Geraldus admitted, as he himself tells and as published by his English translator and publisher, that where people of his day who knew the facts laughed and scoffed at the absurd things he wrote, people of future generations would not know the truth and would not be able to scoff. He said, "People of today laugh at these things because they know the facts, but people of future generations will not know and therefore they will accept them as true history." Thus we see the vileness of a degenerate Roman priesthood employed in inventing falsehoods in order to slander the Irish Church and Nation.

Geraldus also tells us that King Henry did not carry out his part of the agreement with the Pope, whom, of course, he could regard only with contempt and distrust, in that he did not see that Peter's Pence was collected and forwarded to Rome, and that part of it which was collected was put into the King's coffers instead. Geraldus seemed to have bewailed this fact very much as well as the fact that he failed to receive promotion to a

Bishopric from Henry, although he had previously lauded the King to the skies in a composition in which he hailed him as another Alexander possessing the wisdom of Solomon and the very personification of honor and the embodiment of virtue and learning. He also showered praises upon Henry's son John, who succeeded his father as King of England, but, as no recognition or reward came to him from this source, he afterwards related to another cleric that it seemed to be his fate to have to seek reward always from dull-witted princes who never appreciated all he had done to advance their interests with his pen; and that he had praised them beyond their merits, "but that he was never given to telling the truth and could not adhere to it." Out of his own mouth comes the refutation of his fictitious writings, that he was incapable of uttering the truth (*Conquest of Ireland* by Geraldus Cambrensis).

Henry found his affairs at this time so pressing, with his son John in open revolt against him, that, no doubt, even if he desired to do so, carrying out his agreement with Rome was very much more difficult than promising to do so. This agreement between the Pope and Henry is in itself proof that this was Rome's first entry into Ireland as a church, and she entered it as a monster with fire and sword to destroy the one real, true church of the Most High God, as will become apparent.

The people of Ireland were not accustomed to contributing to the support of a foreign church or pope. Their own was the first and supreme Pope Universal. The Roman Pope was but a usurper. It is not my purpose now to relate more fully the history of those times, as it would be irrelevant to the subject at hand, but just so much as will show that Rome and England have had a great and fundamental reason for suppressing knowledge of the past concerning Ireland and the religious worship of its priests and people previous to the advent of Rome and the English invasion.

The Papacy wished to keep the world in ignorance also as to how it had gained its foothold in that country, and, for this purpose, "Saint Patrick" was invented, and in the story was made to connect with Rome back in the fifth century, a story which was pure fiction. The Roman Church's connection with Ireland was brought about through the medium of the English sword and in no other way. The writer, in discussing matters with a priest, happened to refer to Irish literature. He said, "The Irish have no literature." When asked why, he answered, "I cannot speak. My lips are sealed." We are satisfied that Irish Roman Catholic priests have always been aware of this fraud. Church historians have let it be known that Rome merely disciplined the Irish Church in order to make it conform to the proper observance of Easter. But even Bishop Usher on investigation refused to believe it, and was of the opinion that she had far weightier reasons.

The Roman Church has thought herself secure from discovery and exposure from the fact that there was no written record allowed to come down to us, which described in detailed particulars the history of that crime. But the evidence stands strong against her. She has preserved enough of the stolen goods, so easily recognized as such, to convict her. It did not suffice to destroy most priceless treasures of Irish literature, which accumulated through centuries of learning and culture and which she found in Ireland, but she dealt a deathblow to Irish liberty and freedom. That she destroyed so . much literature in Ireland is not to be wondered at. Even if she did not destroy it all, that which she preserved she has perverted and reconstructed, and some of it she has concealed by accrediting it to others. Her purpose was to hide the fact that works and knowledge were taken from Ireland and were the product of Irish genius and scholarship. To spread darkness and ignorance has been her mission from the beginning.

In the year 400 A.D., the Church destroyed the great library of Alexandria in Egypt. She did the same in every center where any great library was known to exist. On the site of the destroyed temple in Alexandria, where the library had been kept, she built a church in honor of "the noble army of martyrs" whom she herself had put to death. She killed them to get them out of her way, then claimed them as martyrs to her faith (Gibbon's Rome, quoted in Bible Myths by T. W. Doane). By such methods and by interpolations and false writings by her priests, from Eusebius down, she thought to keep facts secret from those upon whom she imposed her idolatry. Little did she expect that after the employment of all the cunning known to her priests, who were versed in trickery and backed up by the power, first of the Roman State and later by that of England, that de-

spite all this there would be exposed the villainous part she
played in forging and placing the chains of slavery upon
a great and brave people, whose true and actual history
is great and unrivaled, a people to whom the different
nations of the world of today are unaware of their great
debt.   That the great nations of the world today are
unaware of their great debt to Ireland is to be inferred
from the complacency with which they have viewed her
oppression, with scarcely a protest against the foreign
usurper.

It is all the more to be regretted on the part of our
own country, as a firm stand by our representatives at
the Paris Peace Conference would have secured for her
our oft-proclaimed object in entering the war, to secure
the right of self-determination for small nations. We
have failed in our duty to do the right, and empty
professions are useless. It is good works that count.
The nation that gave us a knowledge of God, of Heaven,
of the Savior, and of spiritual ideals and truth, the Bible
and verities of a future life — that nation is suffering
from civil strife, her territory dismembered, deprived of
her national standing among the family of nations — all
through the effects of a foul conspiracy on the part of
Rome and England.

CHAPTER V

THE BIBLE AN IRISH BOOK ALTERED AND ADAPTED BY BRITISH-ROMAN TRANSCRIBERS

ALTHOUGH our Christian peoples, in the more advanced countries of today, have denounced Jewish pogroms and deliberately planned murders of Jewish people in some of the countries of eastern Europe during the World War, what can they think of the wholesale deportations and murders and suffering inflicted upon the people of what is now called Syria when they know that the Roman Church put her plan in operation to charge them with having crucified the ideal Savior Jesu (The Sun God) and scattered them broadcast over the world. By dispersing those people, she cleared the way for the renaming of places in Judea to make it appear that such a man as Jesus had lived there; that those various places said to have been the scenes of his life and travels were actually real places and in existence on the map with those names. It is something awful to contemplate, but the Roman Church did this thing; and the people whom she punished thus and who bear the undeserved stigma to this day for crucifying the Savior are as innocent of such a deed as the child unborn.

The Roman fathers employed most ingenious methods to establish the "authenticity" of Jesus. To that end they had stories written up purporting to be by certain men, some of whom denied his God-like powers, while there were other witnesses who declared that he worked wonders. Her scribes also wrote up accounts of those who were supposed to be his companions, but written in such a way that their stories would not agree in every minute detail but near enough so that it would not appear that one account was a copy of the other. It must be as a witness giving a different and distinctly individual narration of the facts as seen by himself.

These trained fabricators considered that no two or more persons would write the facts regarding an event in real life in just the same identical words, so it was thought best to have a little variation inserted in the accounts as given by "Matthew, Mark, Luke, and John." So that is how we find it arranged in those four books by the Roman doctors. If Luke tells of an event in one way, John tells it a little differently, and so with Matthew and Mark. Luke records that the miraculous draught of fishes was made at the beginning of the ministry of Jesus (V:6). John says that it did not happen until after he had risen from the dead (John XXI: 11). John says that, although the number of fish was great, the net was not broken; and Luke says that their net did break (V:6).

Matthew says that Jesus told the twelve apostles to go and preach, and commanded them to "provide neither gold nor silver, nor brass in your purses, nor scrip for your journey, neither two coats, neither shoes, nor yet staves" (Matt. X:9, 10). Mark is made to mention the same incident just a little bit different and with a slight contradiction of his "infallible" brother scribe. He says that Jesus commanded them to take nothing for their journey save a staff only (Mark V: 1–8).

Like inconsistencies which are so many in these four gospels stamp them as counterfeit books. In fact, the very names of the authors to whom these books are ascribed are forgeries and misleading. They were intended so to be; for it was claimed that they were "Hebrew," while the plain truth is that they were taken entire from the ideals of the Irish Gospels with the nomenclature slightly changed in order to escape detection.

It is not my purpose to give an extensive elucidation or explanation of the Bible in this chapter or work, but as the Irish Bible and Irish Great Pyramid of Iesa are closely related in spiritual and symbolic significance as agencies and landmarks for the guidance of "wayfaring" mankind in its progress upward toward spiritual enlightenment and regeneration, for this reason I feel I must touch upon this phase in my theme specifically, if only briefly. As I have shown by citations that forgeries were committed, I shall prove by explanations that our Bible is an Irish book, of pre-Roman times, and an out-and-out theft without acknowledgment from the Irish Church of Iesa. Any competent person who knows the Irish language cannot fail to recognize it.

Our present version of the Bible then is an authorized adaptation from the original Irish scriptures with alterations and additions made from time to time by

Roman and British churchmen in secrecy as they deemed it necessary and advisable to do so.

The following agreement in the writings under the names of "Matthew," "Mark" and "Luke," regarding the impression made upon the people by the teachings of Jesus, is an example which shows plainly the work of the forging priests. It would be impossible for such agreement to have occurred in the original writings of any three men writing individually and independently on any subject whatsoever, but in fabrication from the older works and collaborating, the priest-scribes simply blundered and made each of the three "witnesses" write down and repeat the same identical expression in "copy" as to how Jesus impressed the people.

Here is the forged testimony:

Matthew says: "They were astonished at his doctrine" (XXII: 33).

Mark says: "They were astonished at his doctrine" (I: 22).

Luke says: "They were astonished at his doctrine" (LV: 32).

Many authors and critics have commented upon and pointed out the inaccuracies and inconsistencies of the scriptures and many of them have stated their firm belief that they were copied from older books. But none of them could obtain a clue beyond a surmise which was far from the truth and none of them was able to produce the real facts which were necessary to convince. But the work that they did has helped and made it possible to accomplish the desired end. They found so many flaws in it, which the "jugglers" did not cover up, that it kept the question open until the solution was found. The true source has escaped discovery until now; at least it has never before been disclosed to the knowledge of mankind as a whole.

The Irish Scriptures were altered and adapted to the scheme of the church in order to make the fable of Iesa an historical and geographical fact. Names from the Scriptures were given to places in Syria during its occupation by the Crusaders to bear this out. It also suited the purpose of British statecraft to obscure and suppress all evidence of the greatness and culture of the Irish Nation, than whom no people in the world's history have reached greater heights both spiritually and intellectually nor have suffered greater injustice at the hands of priestly imposters or political oppressors.

The men who were engaged in executing this literary fraud committed as well the audacious crime of completely effacing all evidence of credit due the Irish Nation for the most brilliant and glorious service to civilization and human enlightenment. It almost passes belief that a fraud so stupendous could escape so long without discovery. But when we consider the thoroughness and extent to which the plot was carried out, and the magnitude of the forces which were employed in the work, it is not so much to be wondered at, forces such as the Roman Empire, with its world power, then the Roman Catholic Church and the British Kingdom, with propaganda systematically spread abroad in order to create a false impression of everything per-

taining to the past history of Ireland and her people.
These are the forces which have perpetrated and profited by this great fraud. The deception is still continued
and the secret jealously guarded by both the Roman
Church and Britain from the world at large, but more
particularly from the Irish people who have suffered
so much from those two adverse forces. The men who
executed this plot were acting jointly in the interest of
both Rome and Britain. Even to this day, the British
Government does not encourage, even if it will allow,
excavations or investigations to be made about the
hill of Tara in Ireland (Rev. Joseph Wild in *When the
World Comes to an End*).

I will give two citations here, with more to follow,
to show that the names of many of the characters in
the Bible are plainly Irish, and it is because of this fact
that the Irish Roman Catholic priests would not allow
the Irish Catholics to read the Bible. They were told
not to read it, that "it was not a sufficient rule of faith."
The real reason was that some of the Irish people might
recognize the Irish names in a "Jewish" Bible and ask
questions that it would embarrass them to answer
satisfactorily. Nevertheless, it is a very astonishing
thing that what now appears so clearly fraudulent
could have escaped detection for so long a time. There
are three main reasons for this: first, that the people are
slow to attribute fraud and dishonesty to the clergy;
second, that the Irish Catholics who could speak the
Irish language believed, as they were told by the priests,
that the Bible was brought to them from outside in-

stead of being of Irish origin, and, being uninstructed in the principles of man's nature, were not given to investigation or research for spiritual truth; and third, that the field of religious literature has been dominated by the works of professional preachers and other religionists who have kept up the delusion knowingly or who took it for granted that the published accounts of the origin of the Scriptures were, in the main, true and were originally written in Greek with one single copy in Hebrew, as has always been asserted. It will, therefore, be a surprise to Bible readers of today who have had no suspicion of this deception to be told that it was through the medium of the Irish language that the true key would be found for the solution of the mystery of the origin of the Bible. The proof of this fact is here given for all mankind to see and know.

The first of the two citations to be given in this chapter is from the Book of John (Ch. 3, 23d verse). "And John was baptizing in Aenon near to Salem, because there was much water there; and they came and were baptized."

In the latest revision of the Bible, the "Doctors" have altered the word Aenon and have made it Enon. In the older version it is Aenon. This is a compound of two Irish words, Aen, meaning a circle of the Sun, a year, and On, also a name of the Sun. The complete word itself means the Sun. The word On also signifies cause, reason, swiftness, fierceness, eagerness, excellent, noble, good, also wolfdog. These are qualities and attributes associated with and applied to the Solar Sun and to the Sun God by the Aryan or Irish Priests of Iesa. Their theology was based on the idea that the Supreme Deity never had nor has a name. He is known only by attributes, as the "Good" or God, Holy, Most High, etc. And, as the Solar Sun is the center of light and His great representative or "Son" in our system, the Sun God is named after the qualities and attributes of some idea, such as "the Horseman" or "Charioteer," "the Strong One," or "Samson," or "the Fierce One," Horus, "the Heavenly Wolf Who is Eager," swift and fierce.

The Irish, during their sojourn in Egypt, gave the name of On to one of their cities on the Nile. The City of On, the City of the Sun, was afterwards called Heliopolis by the Greeks and Romans. Salem is a "Hebrew" word, but the basis of it is in the Irish word Solas, light. As "Hebrew" is a jargon of the Irish, it follows more or less closely the root it is taken from, as will be seen. So Salem means the City of God or Light.

The meaning of this myth is that John (Aen — the Sun) was baptizing in Aenon, the City of the Sun, near to Salem, the City of God, in the realm of Light, the celestial kingdom. Where else could such a being as the pure and perfected man be said to dwell? In this myth, John, (Aen, Eion, or Ain, three forms of the word and all pronounced Ain) represents the redeemed and glorified man, man at the highest stage of spiritual attainment, next to the Messianic state, so that in his next succeeding life or incarnation here again on earth he will be the Messiah. In the Irish mythic narrative of the Bible we see that, after John, the prophet and holy man, comes the perfected Man-God, the Messiah, Iesa (Jesus).

This is an example of the esoteric truth and wisdom which lies hidden beneath the veil of the scriptural allegory as formulated by those inspired Irish Adepts, and though they have been denied the credit of authorship through a thieves' compact of silence, their wisdom and their works still exist in both the Bible and The Great Pyramid of Iesa.

The second citation to prove that the Bible is Irish, purely and unmistakably so (and I defy contradiction), is taken from the Books of Mark and Samuel.

The Pharisees questioned Jesus because the disciples plucked ears of corn on the Sabbath. He said: "Have ye never read what David did when he had need . . . ? How he went into the house of God in the days of Abiathar the High Priest, and did eat the shrewbread, which is not lawful to eat but for the priests?" (Mark II: 24, 25, 26.)

The first Book of Samuel contains this version of David and the shewbread: "Then came David to Nob to Ahimelech the priest. . . . So the priest gave him hallowed bread; for there was no other bread there but the shewbread, that was taken from before the Lord." (Chap. 21, 1–6.)

The foregoing is but a cryptic allusion to the perfecting work of the Initiate who is engaged in the effort of eradicating from his nature all worldly ambitions and the desires of the flesh for the development of his higher self, the Solar Body, the God within himself.

The word Abiathar, the name of the High Priest, is such a plain and easily recognized Irish word that even the uneducated Irishman or Scotsman, who is able to speak Gaelic, can understand it, and will recognize it at once as a word of Irish or Gaelic speech. It is a compound of two words. The word "Ab" means lord or father, and "Athar" is also the word for "father." The two words combined would literally be "father-father." The literal sense of it would be "Head-Father," for the word Ab is applied to the head of a monastery; but the esoteric sense of it is High Father or God. The vowel letter *i* is introduced to connect the two words into one. The Roman-British scribe in this instance gives us a compound Irish word, and, of course, without the least suggestion that such is the case, makes a play on the name and presents it to us in the English version of the Bible as the name of the "Hebrew" high priest.

It is a priestly deception, as will be seen readily, on the part of the transcriber of Mark, when we understand that the character "David" and the incident connected with him is but a story invented for the purpose of containing an idea, as follows: Abiathar in this allegory alludes to the "High Father God," manifesting spiritually through the Solar-Sun, in his human counterpart, which is the Solar or luminous spiritual body of the initiate "David," who is on the upward path, striving for the victory of the spirit over matter, in the material body or flesh. This should be instructive to every wayfaring man who is traveling Eastward towards the dawn from darkness to light into whose hands these pages may come, as well as to the general body of Bible readers.

The copyist and transcriber who has given us the version ascribed to "Samuel" has "David" go to Nob to Ahimelech the priest. The word Nob is Irish and is spelled Noeb, but it is pronounced as if it were Na-ev, with the *o* having a short sound as *oe*. If the word was written by the priests without the intent to deceive, they would have presented it to us in this form — Noḃ, the dot over the *b* making it *v* or *bh*, which, in the Irish, has the sound of *v*. They have taken advantage of the alphabetical features of the Irish language to perpetrate a fraud on the people of the world. The word Nob means Heaven, sacred or holy. The word Ahimelech means the Heavenly King or Solar-Sun, who is figuratively a champion, hero, or ruler. Melchezedech is another form of the word from the same root. The letter *a* is pronounced broad, as if it were *aw*. The letter *h* is added to it for an aspirate to soften it. Together they form a prefix. "Melech" is the "Hebraized" or jargonized form of the Irish word Miol, an animal or ideal for the Sun. As the Sun moves swiftly, it is in imagination Miol, an animal. It is the figurative name given to the Sun by the Irish priests of Iesa. Therefore, the Sun is called Miolchu, pronounced Melchu, a greyhound. It is also called Onchu, a wolf. Hence, the terms applied to the Sun, "The Swift One,"

"The Fierce One." The greyhound and the wolf-hound have ever been favorites with the Irish and figure in their legends and fables. We see the same deception practiced by the Irish Roman priesthood upon the Irish Catholics of our own day in the word Melcho, a name of the Personified Sun. He is the fictitious person to whom, in the story, "St. Patrick" was sold as a slave. Thus proving to us again that the lying and dishonest priests of Rome wrote a false and worthless history for the Irish people.

· They are the people who stole the ancient Irish Bible and palmed it off on the world as a "Jewish" book, produced by a people over in Syria. It is an invention and an imposture on the world.

The Irish word for wolfdog is On. Hence, the Irish priests of Iesa, during the sojourn of the Irish race in Egypt, gave the name to a city on the Nile. They also applied the name Onchu, the wolf, to the Sun; therefore, we have the "Heavenly Wolf" Osiris, meaning the "High Eastern Sun" (from Os, high, and Soir, pronounced Sir and meaning East, — hence the Morning Sun). He is Horus, "The Risen," from the Irish word Or, aspirated to Hor, meaning a Lord or Savior, one to whom prayer is offered. The word also means "From Whom," in the sense of descent. Hence we find the Horus is the son of Osiris.

In the mythical idea, the Sun is Osiris in the early morning and he becomes Horus, the Risen Sun and Savior, in the early forenoon. He is the wolf Horus at noon when his rays are hot and oppressive, also Typhon, the Evil One. He is the Lord and Savior given to the Egyptian people to worship by the Irish priests of Iesa. Here are the facts that defy contradiction; the Irish language is the treasure house in which these indisputable proofs exist for everyone who wishes to view them. With the truths disclosed in these pages mankind is confronted with a new and altered viewpoint which gives us a new conception of history. The priest and churchman has imposed upon the credulity of the professor. A new perspective opens before us, and scholars and honest minded men and women must address themselves to the task of straightening out the confused and unreliable accounts of the past which have emanated from such obviously self-interested sources as Rome and Britain.

Ahimelech, then, like Abiathar, is God, in his aspect of the Solar King or Sun, whose Divine Human Aspect is the perfected man. Therefore, in this myth, we are told that David ate the shewbread, that is, he received the sacred wisdom of the priests, practiced abstemiousness and self-denial and came into a state of holiness from which he advances to the perfect or Messianic state. And so, from the advancing David, the Messiah is born. Hence, Jesus is said to be born of the "House of David." Thus it is to the Irish Magian Adepts of the ancient religion of Iesa that we are indebted for the knowledge of these esoteric spiritual truths, preserved under the veil of allegory and myth.

The distinction and renown which the Magi gave to Ireland, which island in mythology is referred to as the

"Isle of the Blest," has been taken to herself by Rome, as if it all had come about since her ministration there; hence, the allusion made by her priests to Ireland as the "Island of Saints," that is, Roman Saints. Those great men developed the powers of the soul and became God-like, while their Roman successors have become renowned for their capacity for acquiring stocks and bonds and become distinguished according to their ability as investors.

They have denied to the ancient Irish Masters of Wisdom all acknowledgment of their indebtedness and blotted out so far as they could the very memory of their existence, ascribing their erudition and wisdom to others and they mention them only to traduce them. They covertly refer to them as the "snakes" which "St. Patrick" banished from the island, while the multitude is taught to believe that it was the creeping reptiles of the dust that he banished. The latter never did exist in Ireland (*The Esoteric Club*, by Rev. Canon Lynch of Cork, Ireland). They do not apply to them the dignified term of "serpent," which is the symbol of wisdom, but "snakes" to imply what is low and evil. Baseness could go no further.

The Irish race has suffered humiliation even to this day, through this willful traduction and carefully directed perversion of their history. Fables have been invented and taught to the people as genuine facts and bona-fide history. The writer has, like others, absorbed a lot of their fiction and must confess it was some task to unlearn it and to adjust his mind to the reception of even obvious truths, which conflicted with pious "untruths." It is certainly a preposterous thing to allow a body of pretentious impostors to instill their falsehoods into the minds of the growing youth. Moreover, this political priesthood insults our intelligence by considering themselves solely as "God's anointed" and His special favorites. We are told that in England and Ireland it was the practice to give the priests in many places a number of shares of distillery stock as provision for their "future." The priests speak of their churches as "plants," just as if they were factories, and they are fitted up with slot receptacles to catch any fractional currency which might either by advice or suggestion be enticed from the pockets of the worshipers.

It is safe to say that light is advancing and that truth is progressing regardless of this reactionary force, which is now exposed for the first time in a manner which reveals their plot. It cannot help but open the eyes of mankind to the great fraud, and more especially awaken the Irish people who have been so foully betrayed and sold into the hands of their oppressors.

In the citations which I have given to show and prove that the Bible is an Irish Book, the names of places and the names of characters given show plainly the direct connection with and their derivation from the Irish. The elucidation of "The Great Pyramid" and of the topic "Egypt" will add to this proof, so that anyone who comes with open mind and unbiased judgment will not fail to see it. Every lover of truth, qualified to judge, will be convinced that the names are Irish and only slightly changed in the form and spelling, changed only enough to deceive the unsuspecting. It is seldom that a man arises outside the ranks of the clergy who develops a knowledge of the elements upon which the religious myth is constructed. To solve the mystery of the origin of the Bible, this knowledge and that of the Irish language, combined with a true perspective of history, was necessary. It required also a true insight into Ireland's past and the villainous intrigues of the Roman and British priesthoods and the rôle they played in shaping events of momentous consequence in world affairs. To conceal those facts from posterity, they had recourse to the scheme of falsifying the world's history and substituting therefore a tissue of lies and inventions.

The British propaganda has been fostered by the government Board of Education and such misleading works as Pennock's "Catechism of the History of Ireland" which were put into the Irish school system. Persecution and propaganda have served the purpose intended and have caused the Catholic Irish to place an almost blind belief in the integrity of their priests who are a part of the Roman Church and ably doing the work of Rome in carrying on this deception, while the English churchman has done his part to the same end, namely, to keep knowledge of Ireland's great past history under cover of oblivion.

The Irish Catholics were directed away from a study of the Bible instead of towards it and made to depend on what the priests saw fit to dole out to them.   Otherwise it is reasonable to suppose that long before this day, some Irish-speaking person could not have failed to detect the idiomatic Irish in the very warp and woof of the Old Testament.   It is an undeniable fact that the Irish-speaking Roman Catholics were not frequent readers, much less students, of the Bible.   I have laid some stress on this phase of my theme, but not inordinately so, considering that I am announcing the greatest discovery in the history of all literature, that the Bible is Irish and of Irish origin.   I am aware that this will be a shock and surprise to students and intellectuals in all the enlightened countries of the world, to be shown that they have been made the victims of a fraud.   It was bound to be discovered in time, for truth so evident could not be hidden forever from the minds that were free from bias.   Anyone qualified to approach the truth could not fail to see it, even though the schemers were reiterating their claims through the press and from all the pulpits in Christendom.

There is no doubt in the writer's mind but that the inner circles in British Statecraft and High Church, as well as those of the Roman Church in Britain and Ireland, are keenly aware of this truth and carefully guard the secret of their fraud.   A few years ago, the writer read a History of Ireland by Thomas Moore, the famous poet and author, in which he bewailed the fact that at every turn in his quest for knowledge and facts he found a conspiracy of silence and suppression.   He produced his work under just such discouraging con-

ditions, but he rendered a service to posterity by pub-
lishing his observations of the attitude of those persons
who were in a position to assist him in his search for
facts, had they wished to do so.

My studies and investigations have enabled me to discover facts and truths as presented here and these truths
will stand every investigation. It all goes to prove
that even the cleverest forgers and falsifiers are not
safe from exposure and discovery. So it is the case with
the Roman and British forgers. Although the imposi-
tion of the Savior Jesus, and the substitution of him for
Iesa, brought great riches to the Roman Church, it
required a great and tremendous effort to succeed in
making it appear to the world that he had an actual historical existence.

The people were in a terrible state of ignorance and
superstition, a condition which was favorable to the
Church in effecting this cherished idea. Her ambition
to make that one project alone successful was the cause
of inflicting untold misery and suffering upon the people
of three continents during the wars of the Crusades,
which were instituted for that end. The Roman
Church was obliged to enlist practically all Europe
in these wars. It is estimated that there were two mil-
lion lives lost in carrying out that scheme in the struggle
to drive the Mohammedans out of Syria in the tenth and
eleventh centuries. It was during the occupancy of the
so-called Holy Land by the Crusaders for a period of
87 years that Rome gave the names to the localities
and places there which are mentioned in the Scriptures,

and which names had not been before identified with such places.

During that time they did everything that they thought necessary or that circumstances would permit in preparing the ground to place marks of identification about each locality which was selected to be the birth-place or scene of activity of each of the mythical char-acters to whose fictitious existence special significance or prominence was to be given.

Such, for instance, is the example of the patriarchal character "Abraham" whom they assigned to the "Land of Ur" in Chaldea. Ur is an idiomatic Irish word, and means the Sun, fire, and the East. The word also ex-presses an Irish idea or conception of Heaven. Ur is connected with the fabulous Irish land Tir-na-N'og — the land of the young, or the land of perpetual youth. The meaning of Ur in this instance is fresh, green, plenty, new (not stale or old), liberal, the land of plen-tiousness, the Heavenly Kingdom. And Abraham him-self is most obviously an Irish idea of the personified Sun. There can be no room for doubt as to this fact as he comes from Ur (the Sun), and, to be true to Irish mythic form, each syllable of his name is a name of the Sun. The word Ab is an Irish name for father, and here signifies Father or Creator Sun. And Rah means the moving or revolving Sun. And Am means time, for the Sun is the Governor and Lord of Time and Regu-lator of the seasons. And, furthermore, as Abraham is the Sun, he comes from Ur in Chaldea. Chaldea is a mythical and fictitious name falsely said to be of a

country in Asia. The name is from the Irish word Caul
- (a veil, secret, hidden), meaning mystically the Great
Unseen. A Culdee was an Irish religious ascetic of the
worship of Iesa, a seer.

Abraham has two female consorts, one of whom he
marries. She is Sarah, from the Irish word Sor or Sorc
(Sark), meaning delight, light, pleasure, bright, conspicuous, clear, the day. The other woman was named
Hagar, from the root word Acor, meaning covetousness,
desire. She represents the night. The letter *h* is only
an auxiliary in the Irish alphabet and is used as an aspirate. But the "Doctors" have used it as a regular
letter for deceptive reasons in the formation of the name
of this mythic character. And, instead of using the
letter *c*, they use the *g*. These two letters, in the old
manuscripts, were often used one for the other indis-
criminately.

And so we have Hagar. And, as she is Desire, she is
not Abraham's true wife but his concubine. She bears
him a son, Ishmael (the Irish Ies-Moal). Ies is the
Sun, and Moal means bald. The young Sun, or early
morning Sun, is said to be bald as he has no rays until
later. So Ishmael is the young or morning Sun born
of the Night. So, in the Irish Bible myth, we find that
Abraham, the Sun, has two wives, Sarah the fair one,
the Day, and Hagar the dark one, the Night. Sarah
is jealous of Hagar the concubine and has Abraham
send her away. In the phenomena of Nature, the Day
always sends the Night away.

CHAPTER VI

THE IRISH POPE-KINGS FORMERLY THE RULERS OF BRITAIN

A WRITER in the *Encyclopædia Britannica*, in the article on Ireland, gives a very adroit presentation of when and how the Scots (Irish) were converted to Christianity. He seems to be conscious of the deception that has been perpetrated on the world and that the history of this event could be presented to us in an improved and more plausible fashion than it has ever been done. This deficiency he has endeavored to make up by cunningly mixing into his narrative, in a neat dress, a composition of some truth with fable and fiction. And all in such a manner as to make his story, to the uninitiated, appear like a very "fair" and truthful account. But, now that the truth is out, his story falls flat, although cleverly gotten up and evidently intended to be a very satisfactory summary of Ireland's past. As the *Britannica* is supposed to have weight, it appears to be a good medium for circulating such misleading information.

It is quite obvious that the object is not to tell the truth but to connect up all the better the missing links of the story which his predecessors might have been a little slack about in making it look "right." It would really be amusing if it were not so unjust to see how he tries to "mix up things" by trying to confuse the reader as

85

to the identity of the Scots, the Picts, and the Southern Irish of Munster.

The truth is that they are all of one race and people, and these names have been given to them separately as a part of the scheme to confuse. The nearer to the seat of the great crime the greater the need to confuse any would-be investigators. This writer says: "At that time (314 A.D.) the Irish had possession of many places in west and south Britain, and must have come in contact with Christians. These were more numerous and the Church better organized in South Wales and Southwest Britain, where the Munster or Southern Irish were, than in North Wales which was held by the Scots proper" (*Encyclopædia Britannica*, 9th Ed., p. 247). This is an example of how he tries to confuse his readers by making it appear that there was easy intercourse between the Irish and Roman followers. There was no such intercourse. The adherents of each Church were practically identical with their armies. The Roman Church was only where the Roman spearhead was and nowhere else in Britain. Nor did the Romans lay claim exclusively to the title of "Christians" until, as is said, after 325 A.D., after the Council of Nice. And there was no moving about of the inhabitants from the Roman to the Irish lines. They were kept as much apart as the peoples of the French and German territories during the late World War.

There was no difference in race between the people of Munster, whom he calls Irish, and the same people whom he calls the "Scots proper in North Wales." And there was no difference between those two peoples and the Picts. They were all the same people and Eire or Arran (called Scotia by the priests) was the motherland of the race. The name of Scotia or Scotland has been transferred to Alba, as part of the deception. As there has been a great crime committed and a monstrous imposture put over on the people of the world, they found it to be extremely necessary to write an account of those people that would be confusing, and to change even the local names of places. So those British priests have written up a lot of mythical accounts of tribes and characters with which to do this. It is very easy to see through it when it is explained. But it requires study with the necessary knowledge, at first, to understand it.

The accounts of the early beginnings as given in the histories of Ireland, Scotland, and England, like the early histories of other countries, were all written and composed by the clergy, and for purposes of deception and for the very reasons set forth in these pages. They have done this work under assumed names in order to conceal the fact. And what they have written is a concoction of fiction and fable mostly, that is, so far as real, actual, matter-of-fact happenings are concerned.

The priests who conceived the plan to deceive us, by giving the name of Picts to a tribe of people, took as a basis for their idea a class or order among the Ancient Irish Priesthood of Iesa, who were ascetics. They have called them a tribe and have given them the name of Picts, just as if we today should call the Odd Fellows or Bishops a different race from the rest of the American

people. The word "Pict" means a musician, and
is a camouflaged word for a Druid Priest or Magician,
one who understands sacred magic, or the occult spiritual
forces locked up within the human body. The body is
called the "lyre of Apollo" and he who understands that
instrument is therefore a pict or "musician," because of
certain nerve centers or ganglia through which the
spiritual force energizes. This is why the Harp is an
insignia of the ancient Irish and secretly alludes to
Ireland's distinction and preëminence as the homeland
of the. Magian Priesthood. No other country or people
has such a symbol, and for a good and sufficient reason.

The Irish, previous to the English invasion and the
sack of their church, were called Scots, we are told, not
"Irish" or "Picts," by the Romans. The island had
many names attesting to its spiritual character, but
Ireland was not one of them. This name is a living
testimony to British perfidy and cupidity, for they
conferred this name upon it.

That Ireland was preëminently the Sacred Isle of
"Spiritual" Sun worship, and not the Sacred Isle of
"Romanism," as the Roman priests would have us
believe, can be seen even by the very names of its
provinces. It is figuratively likened to a living being.
Ulster is the head or top of the island, and Munster is
the lowest point or foot; Leinster is the day or dawn
side, and Olnegmach or Connaught is the side on which
the Sun departs or the "nightside of the Sun," while
Meath represents the middle or midriff of the island, or
body.

This writer surely does try to make out that, because there were Roman Christians in Britain in the beginning of the fourth century, there were Roman Christians in Ireland. He cites the fact that there were British bishops at the Council of Arles in 314 A.D. If so, they most likely came from the British territory that had been conquered by the Roman arms and held for the Roman Church, so it is not surprising that they were there, for they were Romanists. None other would have been allowed to live in that territory. They must become Romanists or die. The Irish Church, which was the original Christian Church, was in a struggle for its very life with Rome, and it never surrendered or compromised. Hence, the war to the finish; and false statements, no matter how cunningly invented, cannot alter this fact. Rome has the stolen goods in her possession and she has falsified to the world as to where and how she obtained possession of them. They have set up, and quote from, many false authorities, but to no purpose.

The same writer says that the Irish held many places in West and South Britain about this time, and only legends would show an Irish occupation of a much earlier time (*Enc. Brit.*, 9th Ed., p. 246), and that they must have met many Christians there. Yes, they did come in contact with the Romanists at the sword's point, but not in the manner in which he would have us believe. I may ask, "What were the Irish doing in England at this time in the South and West?" They were there at that time just as they had been there from long ages before, and the Celtic race occupied those islands;

they were ruled by the Irish Pope-Kings who held the Sovereignty of all those islands. They were in the south and west of Britain at this time, because they were already the occupants of the country and were attacked there by the forces of the invading Roman armies who had won the central parts of the country. This writer surmises and builds up false premises on which to put forth further misrepresentations, and he calls upon the writings of other clerics to bear him out, such as "Germanus," "Lupus," "Palladius," "Patrick," and "Colgan," also the "Book of Armagh" and "Probus," etc,, just so much worthless material so far as bona-fide authority or truth is concerned. People are not so credulous today. Times have changed since the day when a Bishop could stand up and tell the people that he had just received a letter from Christ telling them that they must do certain things, and not do other things, as did Eustis, Abbot of Flay (quoted in Richard A. Proctor's *The Great Pyramid*), who told his flock that he had found a letter from Christ that morning on the altar forbidding them to engage in activities on Sunday. Clerical writers, or the bishops, think that they can still "put one over."

It is said that, among the Balkan peoples, the Wallach (native of Wallachia) is the sharpest in a trade or barter of any of the peoples there. He is so clever that the others say that he was born three days before the devil. But it can safely be said that the "Bishop" was born three days before the Wallach. To illustrate — Wallachia is a rocky and mountainous country where Nature has been parsimonious of her gifts to man. Therefore, it is only by great industry and effort that the people are able to eke out a living from those stony hills. But the priest thrives there. He sees to that. There is a superstition prevailing that it is an ill omen to hear a hen cackle at night. The best way to avoid evil effects from this is to bring the fowl to the nearest monastery as a gift. An Irish proverb runs: "If there is a hen or goose, it's on the priest's table it will be." Webster's Dictionary has it that "to deacon" is to cheat, and observation has justified the application of the term. "To bishop" surely means to lie, judging from all the fiction that has been given out under that head. The Bishop is not chosen for his piety or spiritual qualities, but because of his administrative ability, shrewdness, and business qualifications.

The more this writer in the *Encyclopædia Britannica* tries to explain things, the more he unwittingly proves that our facts are as stated, that Rome came to Ireland centuries later than is claimed and then only to usurp, absorb, and destroy. In explaining the status in the Irish Church of the Comarba or the co-heir of the Bishop, as inheritor of both the spiritual and temporal rights, privileges of the spiritual tribe or family, who might be a layman and possibly have sole power fall to himself, he says: "This singular association of lay and spiritual powers was liable to the abuse of having the whole succession fall into lay hands, as happened to a large extent in later times. This led to many misconceptions of the true character and discipline of the Irish Medieval Church" (p. 248).

Aside from the question of whether the office of bishop should be filled by a clerical or a layman, if Rome established her church rule in Ireland about the beginning of the fifth century, as she claims she did, and converted the whole island through the mission of "St. Patrick," and "peaceably and without the shedding of a drop of blood," it is very strange that the Irish people who were so easily converted and who so readily adopted the Roman religion and priests, and who, if this were so, were immediately under the discipline of the Roman Church, should prove so recalcitrant later and have maintained this insubordination all through *medieval* times when Rome is supposed to have full sway there, having according to supposition established her church rule there from five to six hundred years previously. This story we maintain is composed of fiction without a grain of truth. In Rome's history, in dealing with opposition either of a people or of an insubordinate branch of the priesthood, has she been shown to pursue a vacillating or tolerant policy? Quite the contrary.

She did not show much toleration in her treatment of the Huguenots. The massacre of St. Bartholomew will attest to that. She was a demon of cruelty wherever she had power. Did she coddle the Albigenses in the south of France when they refused to subscribe to her beliefs? The Papal Envoy, the Abbot Arnold, gave instructions to the general of the papal army, when the latter said he could not distinguish the heretics from the faithful: "Slay them all. God will know his own."

And, in the course of a few years, there were slaughtered 180,000 souls.

So history itself refutes the claim that Rome was dominant or even present in Ireland and substantiates the claim that the Irish Church had its own rule during *medieval* times, previous to the English conquest. They have invented the pretext "to discipline" as an explanation for King Henry's invasion, but it is merely a "cloak" under which to conceal the purpose and act of conquest of the Irish Church. The Pontiff of the Irish at this time, 1172 A.D., was Galasius. Roman writers claim him as their own under the designation of primate and refer to him as the "saintly Galasius." His name bespeaks his office as the representative of The Sun, from Gal, bright, The Sun. The name is a true and perfect idiom and ideal of the Irish Church Sun worship of Iesa. It does not connect up at all with Rome. In the light of the knowledge which we have today the deception is most transparent. This conquest and its results were the most important events in the history of the Roman Church, and they have been fraught with consequence to mankind. They represent truly the triumph of Might over Right.

The writer in the *Encyclopædia Britannica* tries to make fact and fiction correspond. but without success. The writers of the church have ad no scruples in the matter of altering facts to accomplish their purpose, and did not hesitate to use deception. Wolsey visualized the future when he was Bishop of London, in addressing a convention of the clergy on the subject of the printing press, which was new at the time (1474 A.D.), when he said: "If we do not destroy this dangerous invention, it will one day destroy us" (*Bible Myths*, p. 438, by T. W. Doane). It is in spite of the clergy that light and knowledge have spread.

This writer, already alluded to, says that the differences which existed in the Irish Church, as compared to the Roman Church, were due to Ireland's "isolation" (*Enc. Brit.*, 9th Ed., p. 250). But Ireland was not isolated in those days. It is only since she came under English rule that she became "isolated." Before that time, up to and for long after the Punic Wars, she was the greatest commercial nation in the world, for she was the homeland of the "Phœnicians" (Irish). Their trading ships sailed on every sea, and it is logical to assume, as a natural consequence, that the traders and merchants of other countries also visited "Phœnicia." Ireland became isolated for the same reason that a highwayman kills his victim after robbing him, that there might be no one alive to give testimony against him. It has been the settled and most carefully studied British policy to isolate and misrepresent Ireland. We hope that, as the truth comes to light, Englishmen will be moved to make what amends are possible for the horrible mistreatment and oppression which have been inflicted upon that country. The Irish people have suffered untold misery through no fault of their own, but because they had what Rome coveted for her own power, a Savior, the Bible, and spiritual sovereignty in the Papacy. England was but a tool used by Rome in her striving to attain her end, namely, recognition as the *sole source of the "Divine Authority" on earth.*

The aforementioned writer refers, too, to the question of "Easter," which Rome has given as her reason for the so-called disciplining of the Irish Church. He tells us that it caused a great deal of trouble in the church but endeavors to leave the impression that it never got beyond the limits of a mere polemic affair, a matter of heated discussion. He tells a little of the truth also which will show, as herein claimed, that the Irish Church of Iesa Chriost was the great church of Europe.

He has prepared his ground in advance for this brief but partial admission by saying that these establishments in the countries named were set up by Irish priests who were Christian missionaries within the Church of Rome. He refers to "peculiarities" which the Irish Church had, but says that they were only survivals of what was general at one time throughout the Christian Church and, of course, "Puritan" Rome was shocked at those things. He does not tell what those peculiarities were, but it is a natural inference that they must have been horrible and immoral if Rome could not tolerate them. She does not seem, even in this enlightened day, to be shocked at what her priests have done in the Philippine Islands, in Mexico, or in South America. For that matter, we do not need to go outside of our own country to look for evidence of it. But it is not our purpose to treat on Roman corruption or immorality.

Here is what the *Encyclopædia* writer says on the fictitious alibi of Easter: "On the Easter question especially a contest arose which waxed hottest in England, and, as the Irish monks stubbornly adhered to their traditions, they were vehemently attacked by their opponents. This controversy occupies much space in the history of the Western Church and led to an unequal struggle between the Roman and Scotic clergy in Scotland, England, the East of France, Switzerland, and a considerable part of Germany, which naturally ended in the Irish system giving way before the Roman. The monasteries following the Irish rule were supplanted by or converted into Benedictine ones" (9th Ed., p. 250).

This writer has said much when he admits that the "Irish System" and the Irish monks, under Irish rule, which of course was the rule of the Irish Supreme Pontiff, were so far afield from Ireland as to be in Britain, Scotland, the East of France, Switzerland, and Germany. Even this far would take the Irish monks quite a distance inland into the continent of Europe and proves our statement that the Irish Church of Iesa was there. Is he trying to show that the Irish monks were the sole and only missionaries in those countries converting the people for the benefit of Rome? This seems to be his object. By his statement, the Irish monks would be the preponderant or greatest element in the Roman Church, and were doing a great deal of zealous work for Rome. This could not be so, for we know that Rome was in the field with hostile armies for centuries. This writer fails to tell us what the Romans themselves were doing all of this time. They were trying to crush the Irish Church. Were not the Romans making any converts at all for their church? Were they simply marking time and letting the Irish do the work of conversion for them? His argument is weak and its absurdity needs only to be pointed out.

When this "mere contest," which he would have us believe was all within the Roman Church and "waxed hottest" in England and the other countries mentioned, was settled, why is it that Rome did not make the same changes in Ireland at that time, where she claims to have been established for so long a period, that she made in England and in those other places? Ireland must have been the seat of the trouble. Why did she not change things there? The reason is obvious. She had not been established there, and this writer only makes her course and her guilt appear all the more conspicuous, so much so that all mankind can see it.

Rome, as has been said before, made war on the Irish Church established all over Europe, and, as she advanced with her armed forces, she took possession of the church property and compelled the people to come under her church dominion or be put to death. By forgeries and lies she has tried to make the world believe that these countries were "converted" by her missionaries.

We will let this apologist for Rome speak once more, when he tries to give a little acknowledgment to the Irish monks for what was done by the Irish monks of the religion of Iesa thousands of years before the time he speaks of. He spans a big gap of time and pretends that those Irish monks belonged to the communion of Rome, which, of course, is false; for Rome came in only later with armies to conquer those countries and, by persecution and death, drove out the Irish monks and their successors. Rome appropriated their labors and works and claimed their very virtues as her own. He employs the very same rule which he frowns upon in others, thinking that in this way he can give his story the appearance of being truthful. Rightly enough, he is familiar with Roman methods of substitution and her invention of "Saints" where no saints were. He has made such a creditable attempt at misrepresentation in the foregoing part of his article that he can afford to be "generous" and fair in giving the Irish monks credit; even he himself is misrepresenting the plainest truth.

He says: "Owing to this struggle, the real work of the early Irish missionaries in converting the pagans of Britain and Central Europe and sowing the seeds of culture there, has been overlooked when not wilfully misrepresented. . . . Thus, while the real work of the conversion of the pagan Germans was the work of Irishmen, Winifred or, as he is better known, St. Boniface, a man of great political ability, reaped the field they had sown, and is called the Apostle of Germany, though it is doubtful if he ever preached to the heathen" (*Enc. Brit.*, 9th Ed., p. 250).

This shows us what has been Rome's way of making changes and inventing substitutes for purposes of deception, but the plot is now exposed, I hope, in such plain manner that no one will be at a loss to account for the growth of the Roman Church and the cause of the Roman wars against Carthage and the countries of

Western Europe, such as France (Gaul), Spain (Iberia), Germany, and England. It was to crush the Irish Church of Iesa and to obtain the Popedom and its accessory possessions, the *Supreme* Papacy, the Savior, and the Irish Bible.

CHAPTER VII

The Coming of St. Patrick to Ireland

The story of the coming to Ireland of St. Patrick is an invention concocted by the English priests of the Romish Church, under the leadership of William, Bishop of Malmsbury, who was a dominant personality and well skilled in the arts and trickery of Roman priestcraft and policy. He has been credited, with his associates, as the inventive genius who constructed this purely fictitious, absurd, and mythical story of the conversion of the Irish by "St. Patrick."

St. Patrick is a bogus personage set up to deceive the Irish Catholics. The English high churchmen of today are so conscious of it, and the writer of the article in the *Encyclopædia Britannica* (9th Ed., p. 248) seems to be very much concerned lest he fail to make the bogus Saint appear real in order to keep up the deception. He says: "Our knowledge of the Irish apostle is, however, so contradictory and unsatisfactory that no reliance can be placed on any dates connected with him. In any case, when we remember the time and the state of Europe, it is not at all likely that the place of Palladius could be so rapidly supplied as the above date. (431 A.D. is the date referred to, and Patrick is supposed to be on the scene the next year following.) While there are many lives of the Saint, these are rather legendary than historical

100

biographies. . . . But, although there is much obscurity and confusion in the acts of St. Patrick, there cannot be the slightest doubt of his real existence."

This invention of the character of St. Patrick is consistent with others of which the English-Roman priests have been the authors. A fictitious story has been woven about his name to deceive the Irish, to show falsely the conversion of Ireland and to establish the fact that this conversion was brought about in the day and age claimed, and that it was done "peaceably without the shedding of blood," as the modern Irish are made to believe.

The Irish Roman Catholic priests have ever since kept up this deception. It seems to be a part of the secret understanding between the priesthoods of Britain and Rome. The history of the Saint, or the dates of any of the occurrences mentioned therein, did not need to be very exact, for those plotters held that the more exactly and definite the dates were fixed, the more it would give the story the appearance of having been "arranged" and the easier it would be to contradict it. So we see that the dates were not too arbitrarily fixed nor was even the place of his birth very definitely settled. The English writers claim that he was born in Scotland. The Irish Roman Catholic writers claim that he was born in France. The Irish Roman Catholic priests encourage the belief in the latter place, as if desiring the removal of the birthplace of the "Saint" to a land as far as possible from that of his inception or invention. A priest-ridden people are not in the habit of questioning the facts put before them by those whose authority they consider absolute. Suspicion has never been awakened in them regarding the facts or the deception practiced upon them.

St. Patrick is a fictitious creation from the brain of the English bishop and is based on a myth. The fiction was designed to deceive the latter-day Irish, which it has surely done, and others as well. It is a very simple myth when explained. The idea of the St. Patrick myth is very plain. The fiction of the finding of the three bodies of Patrick, Bridgid, and Culombkill in one grave, which is an aspect of this myth, is symbolical of the triad of the human personality of Spirit, Soul, and Body; Culombkill as the Spirit, Bridgid as the Soul (the Soul is said to be feminine), and Patrick as the Body or personal man.

The Body has ever been said to be the "Grave" of the Spirit. The inventors of this myth had this idea before them in constructing the story and, hence, the fiction of the discovery of the "three bodies in one grave." This invented story has been doing duty as "history" for quite a period of time. It is one of the most important deceits which the British priests have imposed on the world. It has deceived Catholics and Protestants alike.

Another aspect of the myth, like many other religious myths, is that it is based on the Holy Trinity of Father, Son, and Holy Ghost. Be it remembered that Patrick, Bridgid, and Culombkill are associated. As the Higher Triad, Culombkill represents the Father Sun, or Male Principle. Bridgid represents the Mother Principle of deity, the Soul, and Patrick represents the Son. Therefore, he is said to be a "Patrician," one born of noble lineage, as Jesus, the Son, is said to be born of the "Kingly" house of David and is also a "Patrician." This is the first time since it was invented, as far as we know, that this myth has been revealed or explained and given out to the public.

In the story of the mythical "Saint," he is made to accomplish his mission of converting Ireland to Romanism in a most expeditious fashion, "peaceably without shedding of a drop of blood" in the short period of his lifetime. This is absurd in the face of the fact that, in order to preserve her church and papacy, Ireland was engaged in a struggle with Rome for more than one thousand years. In the story of St. Patrick's life, they make a very quick matter of this conversion and even have him perform miracles. They carry this to the ridiculous extent of having him go out into the fields at the request of his sister to gather up some wood for the fire. It happened that it was in the winter season, and the ground was covered with snow and ice. Finding no wood, he simply gathered up an armful of icicles and brought them to the house, where he converted them into fagots for her to put on the fire. Other equally preposterous performances are credited to him. This all serves to show how gullible a people may become through ignorance, superstition, and priestcraft, and proves anew how truthful are the words ascribed to Lactantius: "Among those who seek power and gain from their religion, there will never be wanting an inclination to forge and lie for it." The Roman Church Fathers had a most compelling reason in practicing concealment and, for that purpose, they have tried to destroy all authentic history and to blot out all true accounts of the past records of mankind. They made claim that theirs was a new and original Divine Religion, which, they declared, a specially born Savior and Son of the Great God of Heaven had come to reveal for the purpose of delivering the earth from sin. They assert that He gave this message to twelve poor men who were His apostles. The name of this Savior they called Jesus, and said that he was put to death on a cross, that he had selected Peter as the Head of those twelve men, who, with seventy disciples, formed the new Christian Church. This story is an invention based on and contained in the allegory of the Sun God Iesa and the descent of Spirit into the Body or Man.

This was all taken from the original Irish version of that story and was made known to the whole world long before it was adopted at the Council of Nicea in the year 325 A.D., when the "Christian" Church is said to have been born. The Irish religion of Iesa was the parent religion or church which had prevailed in the countries along the Mediterranean Sea and on the American Continent for thousands of years. Ies, Iesa, Hesiod, and Heezeg Chriost are different forms of spelling the first and second names of this ancient Savior invented and constructed as a myth by the adept Irish priests, to be worshiped by the multitude, the esoteric or secret truths of which were reserved for the priesthood itself. In some cities or localities, the Deity was worshiped under special names, as in Greece the name Ies was transformed into Zeus. Thus the Greeks got their chief god, derived from the Irish Sun God, though its derivation has not been acknowledged by those priests who are aware of the fact. Though some of these priests chafe under the deception, they remain silent and allow the great motherland of Sacerdotal wisdom to be defrauded and denied the credit and honor which is her due.

Some would have us believe that the Hindoos gave Zeus to the Greeks, that the word is derived from the Sanskrit Dyas (Bright Sky). This is not so, for the very reason that the Hindoos themselves got their Sanskrit and their first deities from this same Aryan priesthood as the Greeks did. Dyas is not the chief god of the Hindoos, while Zeus is the chief of the Greek gods. Ies is the Ruling Spirit or God of the Sun and He not only makes the "sky bright" but is the Chief Ruler of our System and the Lord of the Heavens. Aside from the relative distinction ascribed to each, they are both derived from and are a modification of Ies, thus Deas or Dyas, and so Zeus.

It is by just such slight changes or modifications in names that the Roman "Doctors" have formulated the apostle "St. Paul," who is but a personification of the Spirit in the body or the disciple of the Sun God, after the manner of the Irish Church, but not declared to be such. The name Paul is derived from the Irish root word Bel, a name for the Sun. This name changes from Bel to Beul, as in Beul-tin-na (Bel's fire). It becomes Baal, also Ebalus, from this form. In time it becomes Apollo, the Sun God, and by abbreviating this name to Pol they formulated "St. Paul" and made of him an oracle under the new dispensation.

It was this Irish Sun God Ies that was adopted by the Roman Church at the Council of Nicea. At this council, representatives from all parts of the Roman Empire are said to have met at the command of the Emperor "Constantine" to formulate a church policy and unified creed and form of worship which would bring all of the people under one spiritual head. The adoption of such measures would at once increase the power of the church as well as insure the devotion and veneration of the populace for the person of the Emperor, to whom they attributed divine power. The consummation of this policy was expected to be of great benefit to both Church and State, and enable the Emperor to weld the various peoples of the different countries which comprised the Empire into a unified whole.

The Savior Iesa, previous to this time, was worshiped in all of the countries in the western part of the Empire, where he had been preached by the priests of the Irish Church of Iesa for many centuries before. As the worship of the people centered around this Savior Iesa (the Sun God), He was not abolished or denied to the people, but was appropriated by Rome and the name was latinized to Jesu wherever Latin superseded the Celtic language, and has been anglicized as Jesus. It is the history of Iesa that the Old Testament myths have preserved for us. Under the name of Jesu, we are told that He is a different personage, and an allegorical New Testament on the lines of the Old is supposed to represent .

Him in His disguised form. These books are but two versions of the same theme. One is a complement, disguised, of the other. So Rome did not give us a new Savior. She adopted a new policy and gave us only deceit. She has not even given us a new truth. Her claim is refuted by the words of "St. Augustine," one of her own oracles. He says: "The truths of religion existed from aforetime, and were not absent from among men, but from the time of the coming of Christ have been called Christian." "From the time of the coming of Christ" means only since the success of Rome in destroying the early church and fixing a date and location for the Ideal Savior's birthplace.

By the suppression of the facts herein stated, it has been easy for churchmen to preach to people of a modern day and age that Jesus was a new and original Savior, with a birthplace and history as they describe and set forth. This history, I repeat, is borrowed from the mythic story of the Irish Sun God, Iesa. Has the reader a doubt of it? Jesus is said to have been born in "Beth-leh-em," the "house of the day." The Irish word for house is Both. Lah means day in Irish. And as "Hebrew" is but a jargon of Irish, the fraud becomes as plain as "day."

The name Christ is added to Jesus and is meant as a title, which is to indicate that spiritual perfection or the Messianic state has been attained. The name complete is taken from the ancient religion of Iesa and both words of the name have the same meaning. So Iesa Chriost is the name in full of the Irish Savior adopted at the

Council of Nice, and every Irishman who today speaks the Irish language, when speaking the name of Jesus Christ in his native tongue, pronounces it Iesa Chriost, unconscious of the fact that this was the Savior on the cross worshiped by his forefathers for ages even before Rome was founded on her "Seven Hills." In fact and in truth, it was the Irish who founded Rome itself. It was anciently an Irish colony and church establishment, founded by the Finicians (Irish) for both trading and religious purposes. And they gave to it its name, as has been shown by the etymology of the word Rome. Suffice to say that Rome had a most urgent reason for bringing about the Dark Ages and plunging the world into ignorance. This she accomplished by denying education to the people, which policy she carried out to such an extent that in time it reacted upon herself; for, later, the youths who were recruited from among the people to fill the ranks of the priesthood were unable to read or write. When they had occasion to sign documents or papers, they did so by making a mark, thus — X, after their names. These priests were known as marksmen. Only those who were especially favored were able to read and write. From the eleventh to the fourteenth century, Rome devoted her efforts to having fictitious histories written of the different countries, and endeavored to make all of those histories correspond with each other. In this way, the priest-scribes figured that it would be difficult, if not impossible, to discover how Rome obtained her Savior, her Bible, and her religious institutions.

In order to break off all connections with the past, they decided to change the names of the different countries so that no continued and unbroken account of the affairs of those countries would be known to us. This was all in accordance with the priestly axiom that, at the end of an age, when the old religion is overthrown and a new one set up, all trace and memory of the past is blotted out. Thus has Ireland's church and history been submerged by Rome and Britain. And, as if to commemorate and preserve this fact in mythic form, they conferred a name of the island, Erin, upon a daughter of Zeus, — "Eirene or Pax, or the peace which succeeds a military campaign" (*Heathen Religion*, by Rev. John B. Goss, p. 326). It was a somewhat lengthy campaign of murder, outrage, and bloodshed, to be sure, and by this name the English and Roman priests are reminded of it.

New names were given to places so that posterity might not be able to find any clue or evidence with which they might be able to refute any claim or fiction which the Roman priesthood might at any time proclaim as a divine truth. In short, their aim was to leave nothing extant that would serve in any way to lessen in the minds of the ignorant multitude the claim of the fictitious Roman Pope to spiritual overlordship and to be the divine oracle of the Deity, and the claim of the priest to be the mediator between God and Man. Every man must be his own priest before God. There can be no other, for every man must be his own Savior through his own Holy Spirit within himself.

The Almighty God alone forgives sin, and the only mediator or intercessor that man needs, or, for that matter, can have is his own Holy Spirit, or Iesa which dwells within himself, if man merits his higher spirit. No priest can obtrude himself as a third person. It is only presumption on his part to make a pretense of doing so. As with everyone else, he has hard enough task to save himself, that is, to reach final perfection. The institution of Confession is of ancient practice and is older than Rome. It is based on the conception of the idea held by the Irish Priests of the Sun that, as the Sun God saw and heard all things, He knew all things. He was charitable, merciful, and forgiving to all who were contrite and strove to live a better life. As the Sun God could forgive all sin, His priest could also do the same, the assumption being that the disciple has received this power from his Master. But this by no means follows. The practice of this idea served as a discipline among the priests and neophytes and was a potent means in keeping the multitude or laity in subjection to the rule of the priests. It is at variance with modern enlightened ideas as a means to spiritual well-being.

CHAPTER VIII

ROME AND THE "PAGANS"

ONCE the Council of Nicea had terminated its labors in agreement as to the policy and title of the New Christian Church, if entirely new it can be called, and the adoption of the Savior Iesa (Jesu), the civil powers of the state, incited by the priests, began a most rigorous campaign for compelling the people to embrace the new religion. Those who obstinately refused to accept it were put to death, and of those who escaped death many fled to remote places while others were banished from their homes. Terrible persecutions prevailed in all the important centers where priests were active in making proselytes; and it was in the large cities and towns where the new church made its earliest and most rapid gains in numbers, for there the civil powers were strongest and most in evidence. In the rural districts the people were not so immediately under the control of the police power of the government and the priests, and so were not as easily coerced into joining the Roman State Church. They resisted to such an extent that they were held up to the city and towns-people by the priests as objects of scorn and were called "pagans" (from Pagi, meaning "country" or rural people). This is where and how we got our "pagans" of history, — the people living in the country districts

who refused to be forced into the acceptance of the
new creed at the behest of the new political priesthood.
The latter had the force of the civil power at their command and were most unmerciful in their use of it.   The
method employed by Constantine in forcing the people
to accept the State Church is thus set forth:

"The Emperor issued the most severe edicts against
those who were opposed to the new church; at the
same time he conferred dignities and rewards upon
those who professed Christianity, and, instigated by
the clergy whose interest and livelihood were in the
success of the new organization, carried his compulsory
proselyting to such an extent that along with murder
and other cruelties inflicted upon the people, which
did not bring the speedy results he expected, he put
them to the sword, flame, and torture, which did bring
results.   In addition to these methods he offered bribes
to the people to embrace the new creed.   He heaped
honors and favors upon the habitués of his court, who
most naturally were the first to agree with his wishes,
and upon those who were in the civil and military em-
ployments of the government.   He figured on the
common people to follow the example of those of higher
station.   He gave freedom to the slaves and to those
in the ordinary walks of life he gave clothing and bribed
them with gold, and it is said that in a very short time
many thousands of the people joined the church"
(*Bible Myths*, by T. W. Doane, p. 447).

"With the help of the priests, he left no means un-
tried that would further the establishment of the new

order and the suppression of the old. He issued edicts forbidding all others to assemble or to hold meetings, and passed laws that any buildings used by them should be destroyed; and, according to Eusebius, in that way all those who held to doctrines and opinions contrary to the new church were suppressed. Scholars and philosophers were silenced or banished, and their works, all that could be found of them, were thrown to the flames.

"The Emperor Theodosius persecuted with even greater severity, and all writings, wherever they could be found, that did not support or were against the new religion were destroyed" (ibid., p. 447).

And this ambitious hypocrite, this guilty wretch, under the pretense of piety, declared that he could not "allow so much to come to men's ears which tended to provoke God to wrath and offend the minds of the pious."

"The Emperor Theodosius proved himself a fitting instrument for the new Roman project, as evidenced by the acts of his cruel reign. He displayed a vicious zeal in persecuting all those who refused to accept the new faith which he was determined to make the dominant and sole religion of the empire, thereby making the Emperor the complete ruling autocrat of the very souls, as well as of the bodies, of the people" (Bible Myths, p. 448).

So the religion which these Roman despots committed so many crimes to establish should not be called Christianity, but "Romanism" or "Emperorism," in other words "Popery"; for the head of the Roman

State aimed to be not only Emperor but also Pope Universal as soon as the Irish Pope, whose seat was at Tara, could be dethroned. This idea had its birth in the minds of the Roman Hierarchy of an earlier day, and, with the success of Roman arms and the growth of the state, the old religion was made over and imposed on the people under a new name. They wanted a national or Roman religion of their own. So, from the old, they adapted one designed to give them better control over the multitude and still be called "Christianity."

The churchmen, Protestants as well as Catholics, conceal the motive which was behind the new movement and its false claims. Of course, the multitude of our people are not acquainted with the facts, but I am satisfied that the churchmen who are thinkers and philosophers know them well.

An apologist for Rome says (*Enc. Brit.*, p. 227, Vol. VIII, 9th Ed., Article England) : "Christianity is historically the religion of the Roman Empire. Wherever the influence of Rome, East or West, has spread, there Christianity has been dominant, beyond that range it has taken little root." Just so, and as the Roman standard was never planted on Irish soil and the Roman sword never reached Ireland, so the Roman Church power never reached there, and it was not until a later date, in the twelfth century, that at the behest of Rome the English invaders brought it there with its usual priestly accompaniment of fire, sword, and pillage. Not until then was Erin's resplendent light extinguished, her papacy stolen and her Spiritual Sun set into the night of oblivion.

Christianity did not originate in Rome or in any part of the Roman dominions. It is only a false and fictitious assumption to ascribe the beginnings or origin of the Christian Religion to Rome. The period of time which the above quoted writer refers to, and would have us consider as "historical" is a mere 1600 years, that is, from the time of the Council of Nice, 325 A.D., when Rome formally adopted it, until the present time. But the real and true facts of Christianity say that it was the religion of ancient Ireland for thousands of years previous to this date. This was at a time when Rome was but a colony of the Irish Church, the same as the rest of the Mediterranean church colonies or settlements, such as Syracuse in Sicily (taking its name from Soiracus, the Easterner or Sun), which were established there by the Irish Finicians (Sun-Worshipers). This fact is cryptically preserved in the mythic legend of Romulus and Remus, the twin brothers. Romulus is said to have founded Rome, and from him Rome is said to take its name. Romulus and Remus are but two formulated or concocted names of the Sun. Romulus, read backwards, is Sul-u-mor (Solos mor), the great light, The Sun; and Remus, read backwards, is Sum-er, Summer, as it was meant to be. Summer is a mythic ideal, name of and a true aspect of the Sun. These names are taken from the Irish in fact, as well as in ideal. One of the Irish names of the Sun is Somh, Somhra, Summer. It is from this Celtic root word that we get our "Anglo"-

Saxon word Summer. The mother of these twins was the virgin Rea Silvia, the Moon. In the myth the moon is sometimes the spouse and sometimes the Mother of the Sun. These twins are nursed by a wolf — the church — as one of the Irish ideal titles of the Sun was the Wolf, the priests of the ancient church were called the children or brethren of The (Heavenly) Wolf. On earth the church was mythically his spouse. Hence, the church nursed or cared for her priests or children who founded the church colony of Rome. All this at a time before Rome grew strong enough to enter on her career of conquest. As she advanced in growth and power her success made her ambitious.

To possess the Irish Papacy and Spiritual Sovereignty was the motive in all the western wars of the Roman Empire. Those wars were caused by the lust of the Roman Church for power and wealth, for neither then nor since have its professions and practice corresponded. While it has proclaimed as its founder "Jesus," the Exemplar of "peace on earth, good will to men," its history reeks with the blood of millions of human beings, victims or dupes, who were recruited and sacrificed in projects designed to swell the power of that organization. Under pretensions of virtue and zeal for God, the blackest of crimes were committed, all for lust of power and gain. Her history is foul with crime. She counts on time to have it forgotten, and believes that her "historians" will do the rest. They are capable of making some very erroneous statements for purposes of concealment.

I have heard an Irish Roman Catholic priest make the statement, in a lecture on Egypt, that the Mohammedans burned the library of Alexandria in the year 700 A.D. He did but skip 300 years in making that statement. If the truth be known, there was no library in Alexandria at that date to be destroyed. Who could believe that so intolerant and wicked a body as the Roman Church would allow a library to exist in the year 700, in an age when they were putting to death everyone known to have advanced ideas or knowledge? Hypatia, the scholar and philosopher, was put to death in the year 414 by St. Cyril and his mob, many of whom were monks. She was spreading light and knowledge and stood in the way of Bishop Cyril and the reign of ignorance which was inaugurated by the "Fathers." She was seized on the steps of the academy where she delivered her lectures, stripped naked on the street, dragged into a Roman Church and put to death, her body being burned (T. W. Doane, *Bible Myths*, p. 440).

For more than a thousand years thereafter, it was more than anyone's life was worth to have it known that one could think for oneself. It was a long cry from Hypatia to John Huss and Galileo and the victims of the Spanish Inquisition. The Roman Church policy did not tolerate or encourage libraries any more than it tolerated the Irish Church of Iesa. A church that is spreading ignorance and suppressing knowledge is not suffering libraries to exist. This priest would falsify in order to remove the blame from his own church and place it upon another. His church committed this crime under the leadership of the zealot St. Cyril, Bishop of Alexandria, in or about the year 400. The following excerpt, taken from the writings attributed to "St. Augustine," will show how much reliability can be placed upon what they have written for us. "Augustine" is said to be one of the greatest of the church fathers. He says: "I was already Bishop of Hippo when I went into Ethiopia with some servants of Christ there to preach the gospel. In this country we saw many men and women without heads, who had two great eyes in their breasts, and in countries still more southerly, we saw people who had but one eye in their foreheads" (quoted in Taylor's *Syntagma*, p. 52, found in *Bible Myths*, p. 437). A people for whom such things were written must have been grossly ignorant or reduced to a juvenile state of mind. In our day children ten years old would refuse to believe such stories. I have quoted this to give an idea of the mental soil in which "Romanism" developed and can best flourish, and this is a sample of what "one of the greatest fathers of the church" wrote. This statement of "Augustine's" is pure falsehood, but no more so than the story given out by those same "Fathers" as to the real source whence they obtained Jesus and the Bible, the story by which they have deceived the entire Christian World, saying that they came of the "Hebrew" race, a race which never existed and which was but a priestly cult or order of the early Christians of the Ancient Sun Worship of the Irish Religion of Iesa.

CHAPTER IX

THE FICTION IN ROMAN HISTORY

IT has been said that the history of ancient Rome is mostly fiction. This observation is very true. But, in the absence of any special effort to expose these fictions, they have persisted through the efforts of modern churchmen and have been embodied in the history textbooks of the schools. These invented stories of events are still taught as genuine facts. This fiction is not due to our authors having merely a misunderstanding of the past or but a partial knowledge of the events of those remote periods, but it is the result of a studied propaganda which has been carried on by Rome and Britain for centuries. The operation of this propaganda has been continued in full force because the ruling spirits of the Roman and English church hierarchies are as alive to the fact and as conscious today of the fraud perpetrated on the world, resulting in the overthrow of the Irish Church and the false story of the Irish Bible and Savior, as they were at the time the fraud was first enacted. As Rome and Britain together brought about this state of affairs, they both have ever since endeavored to keep in circulation the false and absurd tales which they invented and presented to us as history. In fact, our history of Rome has come from the English hierarchy and was composed to harmonize with this idea. The internal evidence alone is sufficient to prove this, even though other evidence were lacking. No matter how wide the rift has become in politics and religion between England and Rome, since the perpetration of this great crime, their joint guilt and the fear of the consequences of exposure have been the impelling motives for maintaining secrecy. The very life and existence of the English and Roman churches depended upon a truce regarding this matter.

The English Church prides itself as being the eldest daughter of the Roman Church and, therefore, an "Apostolic" Church, a claim which is as false as that of Rome itself. Both Peter and Paul, as well as the rest of the so-called apostles, are but ideas personified. They never existed as human beings and are but invented characters. The lesson taught by the manner in which the "mother" church, Rome, acquired the Papacy was not lost on the "daughter," for in due course of time and with the development of events, the idea was born in the minds of the English hierarchy that some day the English Church would displace the Roman and appropriate the Papacy for itself and become the ruling church of the world. Is not this the real reason why King Henry VIII was proclaimed head or Pope of the English Church? They were conscious of the fact that it was by force of English arms that Rome got the Papacy and they thought that the time was at hand for them to reach out for it. Rome had become to them as a model. It was a time when Eng-

land was deeply conscious of her position and importance, and the idea was held that England was destined to be the logical successor of the Roman Empire
as a world power. To this day she has not relinquished
that idea. It is an ideal which she is secretly and
steadily pursuing.

The English State has persisted in its endeavors to
extend its dominions with the idea of dominating the
world. The Papacy was to be an aid to that end. They
knew how Rome acquired it, for they had reduced and
plundered Ireland in order to confer it upon her. Now
they thought the time auspicious to appropriate it as
an appendage and aid to the English crown. But this
ambition was destined not to be realized. The course
of events has kept the Papacy at Rome. However,
the British State has persevered in its efforts to extend
its empire to this very day. In England, Church and
State work hand in hand and "My Lord" Bishop still
sits in the House of Lords participating in the acts of
vicious government as evidenced by the recent happenings in Ireland. A certain bishop in the upper branch
of parliament defended the killing by government
forces, whose deeds, said to be justified as reprisals,
have been denounced by an outspoken portion of the
British press as a disgrace to civilized government.
The propaganda of British Church and State is carried
on in our own country. It is very evident in the tone
of our leading newspapers. In our school histories it
is carried on in one of its phases, in the guise of fabulous
events which are presented as real occurrences in the

history not only of England but also of Rome. The
same can be said of the history of Greece, for the authorship is the same and for the same purpose of deception.
It is not within the scope of this work to do more than
give a few succinct examples.

In writing their histories of Rome and Greece, the
church scribes had no intention of confining themselves
to the narrative of actual facts which did happen or might
have happened in the material and political development
of those two countries. If they had really wished to
write an accurate history of those countries at the late
day in which they were composed, it would have been
almost impossible to have done so, for in the beginning
of a certain period which those histories treat of and
for centuries later, the Roman Church was engaged in
the destruction of libraries and records rather than in
preserving them. All the histories written by the priests
and monks were falsely colored and intentionally fictitious. They were written to convey a secret meaning
to the "chosen ones." Were it not for the facts presented in these pages it would be difficult to reconcile
the action of the church in destroying all literature and
records in one age, and at a later period manifesting
such zeal in endeavors to encourage the production of
literature and "histories" and the establishment of
schools in which to give instruction in those histories.

Those histories were written for purposes of propaganda, which is still being carried on. The English
invasion of Ireland at the behest of Rome, the suppression of the Irish Papacy and Church of Iesa, with the

appropriation of its Bible and Savior, and the false statements made by Rome as to the Savior's birthplace and earthly career, made it absolutely necessary for church writers to produce "histories" which would either substantiate the fact or make it very plausible or difficult to refute. So, therefore, they have given us an ingenious account of the past ages and blended in the fictitious stories of the birth of Jesus and how we came to have the Bible. In writing their histories, they have invented and introduced such "facts" as were suitable to contain certain hidden ideas and at the same time serve as a history for the multitude.

Along these lines they proceeded to reconstruct history. After the plan was thought out, the absence of real facts presented no difficulty to the writers. They invented the facts which would best serve the purpose they had in mind. These facts conform to certain mental conceptions of the writers and represent aspects of man's physical or spiritual nature, or both as the case may be. The interpretation of the historian Buckle will explain the philosophy and lines upon which the priests of Rome and Britain built up their histories. He says: "The real history of the human race is the history of tendencies which are perceived by the mind, and not of events which are discovered by the senses." Either through instruction or by intuitive penetration, Buckle became aware of the process or lines along which our histories have been written.

Let us consider the mythical personage "Julius Caesar," who has been introduced into Roman History

by the priests in order to glorify Rome with great characters. While at first they endow him with the qualities
that make him very human, they finally elevate him
to the magnitude of a demigod and, at death, deify
him. As a hero leading the Roman legions, he represents, like Hercules, the Sun God. When he crosses
the Rubicon to make himself master of Rome and seize
the crown, his character changes. Here he represents
the spirit or human ego of man being born into the
flesh and taking possession of his body. One of the
definitions of the word Rome is "Body," and the Rubicon, ruby or red, represents the blood in the body.
This illustrates the priestly ideals on which false history has been written. This also explains why they
say that the month of July was named after Julius.
It was named for "Him," but long ages before he became a Latin hero. The name of the month of July
is taken from the Irish name of that month, which is
Iul (there being no J in the Irish alphabet). The word
Iul represents the Sun in his aspect of power at that
period. As the Latin is a daughter of the Celtic, the
British priest-scribes borrowed the name and created
a new Roman ·hero and demigod, "Julius" Caesar.

Forging history was a practice with which the British
hierarchy had long been familiar. At a later date,
with the assistance of Irish monks and scholiasts, they
wrote the works which were attributed to one William
Shakespeare, for the same purpose of creating for
England what they had already done for Rome, namely,
to give her an illustrious son, a transcendent genius

for emulation and admiration of future generations. Critics have noted the form of expression and language used by "Shakespeare," peculiar to the English spoken in Ireland rather than that which was spoken at the time in England, without drawing the inference that those works, or some of them, were written by Irishmen. They were merely struck by the peculiarity of the words (brogue) used in Ireland and were in nowise suspicious or aware of the purpose of the hierarchy. They did not connect the monks and scholiasts with the works. The works bear strong internal evidence of Irish production, and were given out later as the products of the genius of Shakespeare with less fear of successful refutation in England. Their only fear of exposure lay in admissions made by someone from within, someone conversant with the plot and purpose of it all. This accounts, we believe, for the real cause of the death of Bacon, who was high in the Council of State, by the unscrupulous court cabal. This hierarchy had visualized Britain as the great ruling world power, and their purpose was to create a "genius" to correspond with England's ambition and exalted position. How well they succeeded is evident to all. Victor Hugo declared that Shakespeare was the chief glory of England. But their selection of a personage or character upon whom to father the result of their labors was a poor one. They had no idea at that day of the widespread diffusion of education, culture, and literary discrimination of the succeeding centuries. They attributed their works to a "personage" who did not measure up to the "gift" bestowed

upon him. Despite all the assertion and reassertion of
British writers to the claim that Shakespeare was the
author of those works, they have never been quite
able to convince the world of it. Until now, it has remained an open question. Those who have accepted
it are those who are prone to accept any fable or fiction
emanating from the clergy without question, as they
accepted their version of the story of the origin of the
Bible and Savior. But discriminating and thinking
persons refused, and rightly so, to accept the claim
made that the uneducated and untutored actor was the
author of those works which contain such evidence
of knowledge so intimate and varied, as well as of ex-
clusive associations which were beyond him. The
deception has served the purpose it was intended for,
to exalt English national self-esteem and reflect honor
upon England, and to serve as an example for future
generations of Englishmen to emulate. Such deception has even been practiced by our American biog-
raphers, but in lesser degree, and from a similar motive,
to stimulate American youth to emulation, by writing
into the life of George Washington that he "never told
a lie." This idea which furnished the motive for the
deception of those works is a potent one, and still is an
important factor in the policy of British statecraft.
This can be seen in the sentiment expressed by the King
at the recent exercises over the new government building for the London County Council. This structure
cost, according to the press, the sum of $17,000,000,
an enormous amount. But the king, in justification

of this great outlay, said that it would "stimulate the development of that sense of citizenship which it is so imperative to cultivate." So the effect sought after through the substitution of those works is most obvious, the stimulation of English consciousness and national pride, and the glorification of England before the world. Those works are a "wine of rare vintage" and they reflect the rich and ripe wisdom of the prime philosopher and scholiast, which "Shakespeare" the actor was not. Such ripe wisdom has ever been, from time immemorial, associated and identified with the cloister. It is but a piece with other deceptions emanating from the same source. The character "Shakespeare" is too weak to bear the mantle of "Toth." His selection was dictated by ambition and zeal rather than sound judgment, to say nothing of honesty. It is but an old and familiar ruse made use of by the British hierarchy to laud England.

To get back to Rome — "Augustus" Caesar is also another fictitious character formulated to glorify Rome and commend her to the admiration of mankind for the noble characters she had produced. Augustus also represents the Sun. Let it not be forgotten that the ancient Irish were the "Hebrews" and worshiped and idealized the Sun God. The Roman Church, cruel and murderous, by means of the sword, succeeded the Irish Church and has continued the idealization and worship of the Irish Sun God Iesa Chriost under the name of Christianity. Augustus, then, represents the Sun in the month of August. In the story, or forged history, he is known by his ordinary name of Octavius, the "eighth," for August is the eighth month of his course in his annual revolution. When he is crowned "Emperor" or ruler, he is called Augustus. The priests have him reign for "forty-four" years and, as he is getting old and feeble, he has a campaign on his hands against the German tribes in the "North," where the Sun's power is weak. So he sends his general, Varus, a fictitious character (from the Irish Vara, meaning shaved, implying that the Sun was shorn of his rays, loss of power, the impotent Sun), who is defeated in the North in an engagement with the Germans in "Teutoborg Wood" (denoting loss of virility). When news of this disaster reaches Augustus, he is made to exclaim, "Oh, Varus, Varus, give me back my legions." This loss of power he must have felt keenly; as he is feeble now and infirm, they have him lay down his burden and expire gracefully as the September month is at hand, when the Sun's power perceptibly declines. He is also deified.

And this is Roman History, written by the priests to cover up Roman misdeeds, and intended to divert the minds of posterity from contemplating the awful tyranny, slaughters, suffering, and spoliations which were enacted during the period of Roman rule. It also flatters Roman vanity, and Augustus finds many admirers, especially among the English churchmen who are as occupied as ever in keeping up the delusion and deception.

In this Augustus myth, we see again ideas borrowed from the mythology of the Ancient Irish system of building up heroes and demigods personifying the qualities and attributes of the Sun God. As is shown, they have used the Irish names as they thought that, as the Irish language was dead and its literature destroyed, there was no fear of the deception being discovered.

Another falsehood is the myth introduced into Roman history by the priests in regard to the fictitious tribe called the "Vandals." There never was a tribe of that name. It is an opprobrious name introduced by the British-Roman priests and secretly intended as a term of execration for the Irish Church, Rome's opponent. It must be borne in mind that there had been a war which lasted for centuries between the Roman and Irish churches in the endeavor of the Roman Empire and Church to acquire the Irish Papacy and dominate the world. In their histories priests and churchmen allude to this struggle in a covert manner, and refer to the adherents of the Irish Church as Arian Christians, that is, the followers of one fictitious Arius. They are said to have been a "schismatic sect," but as a matter of fact they were the first and original Christians from time out of mind, as the Irish Church of Iesa was the original "Christian" Church. As the Roman Church, by the aid of the English sword, finally prevailed, her historians have covertly introduced slanderous terms to apply to the Irish Church. For this purpose, they have given to "history" that strange and elusive tribe of barbarians that are said to have invaded Rome, and which impartial writers or investigators have never been able to discover. In fact investigators have not

been able to find who they were or what had become of
their descendants. Their identity has been lost. The
name Vandal is but a calumnious term used by the
Roman Church writers to apply to the early Christian
or Irish Church and its adherents who resisted the authority of the usurping Roman Church. At the period
of time that the Vandals are made to appear in the
story, the Germans belonged to the Irish, hence the
"Arian," Church and were its militant upholders. The
Roman wars against the Germans were primarily for
religious conquest, and were but a continuation of the
age-long struggle between the two churches. It was religious motives that impelled the Germans to undertake
the conquest of Italy and Gaul as a reprisal against
Rome's invasion of Germany and her attack on the
Irish Mother Church. And, although the Roman
Church prevailed in the end, she had to endure the loss
of her physical power, the Empire, which was overthrown by the supporters of the Irish Church.

Since that time, in the succeeding centuries, the Roman
Church has played a despicable part, through bribery,
trickery, and diplomacy, in her endeavor to reacquire
that lost physical or temporal power, by playing off one
prince against another. Nor did she stop at forgeries
to that end, for example, the documents known as the
"Donations of Constantine" and the "False Decretals,"
which were forged to bolster up her claim to the temporal
power by showing that Constantine, when he withdrew
to Constantinople, left her the sovereignty of Italy and
the West. The subterfuge of the "script" or written

word she has never hesitated to use for her deceitful and dishonest ends. She keenly felt the loss of the temporal power in her efforts to exact tribute from the people of the different countries and in her efforts to keep their rulers subordinate to her will. This loss of temporal power was particularly felt during the period of the Reformation. If she had had it at that time, the succeeding history of Europe and the world would have been another story.

The term "Vandal" signifies "desire." It is formulated from the Irish word "andal," desire. In Irish the word "van" signifies woman, therefore the "woman of desire or lust." The priest or church is ideally supposed to be at war with "desire and lust," and, as we speak of a church in the feminine gender, this term has been scurrilously applied to the institution of the Irish Church, on which "virtuous" Rome made war. Thus the Vandals are a tribe invented and embodied in our histories for purposes of secret British and Roman slander against the early and original Christian Church, a church whose traditions of godliness and virtue have come down to us and, without their identity as a body or church being known to them, have been the inspiration of the zealous among the Protestant Christian denominations of Europe and of our own country.

At the period we are speaking of, Rome was entirely engrossed in war with the German tribes, and we can follow the "Vandals" very easily. The German tribe of the Visigoths or Western Goths, invaded Spain and they were the only German tribe that made conquests in that country. Their descendants could be traced among the light-complexioned Spaniards for generations afterwards. And the naming of a province in Spain "Andalusia," after those Germans, shows for whom the term was intended and the purpose as stated above. But for the camouflage, the church scribes have made the "Vandals" cross over from Spain into Africa, the mythical region of desire and lust, and establish an empire there. After a time they make a foray in their ships against Rome, which they capture and plunder. They carry away great loot with them back to Africa in their ships under their leader "Geiseric," the posterior (from the Irish word geiser). And this is "Roman" history as well as British propaganda which has systematically slandered the Irish Nation and Church.

The Vandals are said to have remained in Africa a period of one hundred years, at the end of which time the Emperor of the East, Justinian, sent his general Belisarius (the Sun) to drive them out of Africa. In the "historic" narrative, their descendants became quickly absorbed by the surrounding population and in a few generations they disappeared from view, not a trace of them being left. This lying slander is secretly meant to convey the impression, through the leader "Geiseric," that the Irish Church was a church of Sodomy. They have not merely stigmatized the first and true church and its adherents, by calling them Vandals, but they have persistently laid such emphasis upon it, that the term has become a synonym for all that is cruel, barbarous, and destructive. In this way they have given to fiction the appearance of fact. Our histories are sadly in need of honest and enlightened revision in order that this Roman and British fiction may be eliminated.

For the myth of Constantine we are indebted to the spurious historian "Eusebius." He is used as the authority for ascribing a vision to Constantine in which he saw a fiery cross in the heavens, with the words "By this sign conquer." The priestly fabricators, who have written all the history which has been allowed to exist and come down to us from those times, have made a special miracle for Constantine out of an everyday occurrence of the Sun's appearance in the heavens. It is a natural phenomenon that on every bright day the Sun, as it proceeds on its course, can be seen in the form of a cross in the sky. Any person can see it once the attention is called to it. It is seen in Midsummer, in the Spring and Autumn to the best advantage. Constantine is made to see it on the 27th day of October, on which day he is said to have defeated in battle "Maxentius" who ruled Rome as Emperor jointly with him. These things and personages are purely mythical and are taken from the Irish mythology. Con is an Irish demigod or Sun God. He is one of the mythological Irish Kings. He is Con of the "hundred Battles," King Con-cu-Bar, son of the Heavenly Wolf, or Sun God. As Rome stole the Irish Bible, Savior, institutions, and traditions, as well as nomenclature, she stole also the name of one of the greatest of the Irish heroes. to be founder of her church.

Maxentius is a fictitious personage also, and the name

is a compound of Latin and Irish, spelled in camouflaged fashion, and alludes to the evil one. Max means great, and Antias is a name of the "Devil," really meaning great heat, from the aspect of the Sun in midsummer when its heat is oppressive. An-tias, the heat or great heat, is Irish or Celtic. Hence, Maxentius, the "fiery Sun," loses its fierce heat by the 27th of October, and Con, the Genial Sun, again reigns overhead. So we see here the secret allusion of the mythical adoption of the Irish Sun God "Con" by Rome and making him the founder of the "Christian" Church under the title of the' Emperor "Constantine." The British have featured this myth also with the allusion to the fact that Britain assisted Rome in bringing it about, as we find this fiction woven into the story that Constantine's parents were the Emperor "Constantius" and his wife, Queen Helena, who came from Britain. A wife is always an assistant and helpmate to her husband, so in this royal pair we have the two mythic characters doing duty as sponsors for their offspring, the mythical founder of the Roman Christian Church: Con, the Sun God, and Helena, the Moon. The Moon is always said to be the spouse of the Sun.

That the church authorities, who have appropriated this "personage" to whom to attribute the founding of their Church, acted consciously and with intent, in so. far as to the character which he was meant to represent, may be well understood by what Dr. Draper says regarding the honors paid "Constantine." He says: "His statue on top of the great porphyry pillar at

Constantinople consisted of an ancient image of Apollo, whose features were replaced by those of the Emperor, and its head surrounded by the nails feigned to have been used at the Crucifixion of Christ, arranged so as to form a crown of glory." Apollo is the Sun God.

This clearly shows the false basis on which the claim of Rome rests. The name of her so-called founder for obvious reasons was not made use of until after the conquest of the Irish Church when she appropriated as a part of the spoils the name of the mythical Irish Demi-god and Hero-King, the Sun God Con, and for effect changed the name of Byzantium to Constantinople. This, we believe, is the truth beyond the possibility of contradiction. This explanation makes it easy to understand why Lord Macaulay, the English historian, so strongly commended the work of another English writer, Gibbon, by saying that "all who would write on Roman history, must go back to the foundation laid down by Gibbon." All of which shows how thoroughly they have endeavored to establish a belief and confidence in an authorized version of history, ingeniously composed of a good deal of myth and fiction, and caused it to be accepted as fact.

The events in the life of the Emperor Constantine are written so as to make his life read like the narrative of a series of incidents which might happen to a human being in such a rôle as that ascribed to "Constantine." And, as to his "vision," the "Cross of Light" in the heavens is an aspect of the Sun's appearance which was well known to the priest-scribes. In the morning, before the

Sun reaches meridian height, by half closing the eyes, one can see the great shaft of light streaming forth from the luminous orb toward the earth. This forms the upright staff of the "Cross of Light" and on either side of the globe of the Sun will be seen a great arm of light which forms the horizontal beam of the cross. Constantine's being made to hear the words spoken, "By this sign conquer," is suggested to the creator of this myth by the fact that every human being is in the form of a cross, to correspond to the Solar Orb. For when a man stands with body erect and arms extended laterally, he is in the form of a cross. This is where the mythmaker got the suggestion for his idea and it is in this human body, shaped like a cross, that the ego or self must conquer his own lower nature, animal passions, appetites, lust, selfishness, and all other sinful qualities, in order that he may build up and become united with his luminous solar body, the spark of divine essence which is vouchsafed to every human being who will strive, by living a pure and enlightened moral life, to attain it, even though it requires many incarnations to achieve perfection, or union with one's God, one's higher self.

Eusebius has been called the "father of lies," but it is not at all certain that such a man as Eusebius ever existed. His name has been useful to Roman Church "historians" in order to have someone to whom they could attribute sayings and writings which might have been and were written long afterwards, as it was a long and laborious task which Rome had to perform when she undertook the fabrication of history, both church and secular, that would be successful in deceiving posterity in all succeeding ages. This was set forth in a letter from Thomas to Gregory when he said that "Some were prone to censure and find fault with the work of the fathers, but for my part, I am of the opinion that instead of finding fault with them, that their work should be commended with great praise, rather than condemnation, considering *the difficult nature of the work that they had to do*." An idea of the method they employed in forging both history and scripture may be gleaned from the account left us by Bishop Faustus, who expresses his opinion in this wise: "It is certain that the New Testament was not written by Christ Himself, nor by His apostles, but a long while after them, by some unknown persons, who lest they should not be credited when they wrote of affairs they were little acquainted with, affixed to their works the names of the apostles, or of such as were supposed to have been their companions, asserting what they had written themselves was written according to these persons to whom they ascribed it" (quoted in *Bible Myths*, by T. W. Doane, p. 460).

Rome has always appreciated the value of the *Written Word*, and the "Book" is a hoary institution, an adjunct to the priestly cult, to which the unsophisticated give great credence. Therefore, for a long period of years, staffs of monks and priestly scribes were maintained in Rome and Britain, writing and composing false history to cover, not only the so-called early beginnings of the church, but of all the profane history of earlier times, in order that it might correspond and not conflict with the

allegories of the Bible, which book, while it remained
with the ancient Irish priesthood, was a record of spiritual
idealisms and characters. When Rome appropriated
this book, she strove at once to make of it a history, and
to give Iesa a realistic and historical career. So the
names in the Bible, of places which had simply a secret
allusion to spiritual things and human qualities and
conditions in man, in his progress from the animal to the
spiritual state of perfection, were given a different
meaning and were converted into bona fide history.

Thus, with a shrewd conception and understanding of
policy, Rome gave to the Irish Bible a history and a
geography which, through her efforts to give it the
appearance of truth, as a record of actual occurrences
and facts, have heaped woe and misery upon mankind.
To perfect this project Rome preached and instigated
the wars of the Crusades. This was for the express
purpose of getting possession of the countries of the East
and to give names to places in this country called "Palestine" or Syria to correspond with the allegorical and
cryptic names, Irish names, in the Bible. And Irish
names they are still to this day, and this is the main
reason why the Irish Roman Catholics of our day were
not encouraged to read or study the Bible. It was
because of this, too, that the Irish language was mainly
suppressed and all but destroyed. To carry out this
scheme of keeping the knowledge of these things from the
world, Rome has conveniently invented a list of fictitious
historians, names which the priests assumed in order
to set up "authorities," supposed to have lived in the

periods of time assigned to them, and who would be cited by posterity to verify the falsifications which they had established as facts. Such are the names "Herodotus," "Manetho," "Berosus," "Josephus," "Irenius," "Origen," and "Eusebius." These "historians" appear, in the light which we have today of her doings, as so many fictitious personages to whom to attribute writings which were done by the Roman and British priests of much later times. They were very busy concocting history after the English invasion of Ireland and the conquest of the Irish Church, and right away in the early part of the thirteenth century they set about altering the Irish Bible to make it their own. This revision or alteration took place about the year 1208 of our era. King James' agents have tried their hands at altering it since then and it has been "revised" again in our day. At the time of this writing, the public press gives notice, under date of May 22, 1922, that in the Presbyterian Convention held at Des Moines, Iowa, there was a movement on foot for a "shorter Bible," but it failed of adoption. So the original Irish Bible has been tampered with and altered from time to time, according to the interests or purposes of those able to do it.

CHAPTER X

Hebrew a Sacerdotal Dialect Improvised from the Irish Language for the Secret Use of the Priests

A MYSTERY once explained is a mystery no longer. Yet, I hold that the solution and explanation of the Bible origin is of vastly more interest and benefit to mankind than to allow it to remain a secret and a mystery. Intellectual mankind needs to know the truth; fables or fiction cannot be substituted for it, nor will the great mass of inquiring minds concede that the clergy is the only class that is entitled to know the truth — when it can be acquired — while the multitude may be regaled with fables and myths. It was in the spirit of this latter idea that the English churchman, Dr. Burnet, wrote his treatise, "De Statu Mortuorum," purposely in Latin, to instruct the clergy only, not for the benefit of the laity, saying that "too much light is hurtful for weak eyes" (*Bible Myths*, pp. 436–7).

We do not agree with him in the sense that he wished to deceive men. Our purpose is to enlighten, and the proofs already given cannot be disputed or contradicted. The Old and New Testaments are just copies, transcribed and made over and supplemented with additions, from the ancient Aryan Gospels of the Elder Magian priesthood of Aryan (Erin).

I know that the Christian World will be surprised to learn that it has been so grossly deceived and imposed upon by Roman and English churchmen in this matter. Deception of the people as a policy was a principle on which both priesthoods were in hearty accord, much as they differed on denominational lines or in allegiance to different religious rulers.

However, we have given out the real truth and it cannot be denied, gainsaid, or explained away. The proof is now given out. It is as open and as plain as day for anyone who will take the trouble to investigate. Only a public ignorant of the Irish language could accept such a barefaced fraud. I declare that anyone who is at all competent to examine the facts as herein stated will be astonished to find it possible that such a lie could find credence. Under any other circumstances, only universal ignorance of the true facts could bring it about. Hence, the Dark Ages were ushered in through the instrumentality of Rome and Britain. The very Bible names prove it. So also does the name of The Great Pyramid prove that it was built by this same order of the Irish Magian priesthood, the knowledge of which has also been suppressed.

The Irish Scriptures were palmed off on the world by Rome, with the aid of British priests who translated them into Greek in order that it might pass for the original tongue in which they were composed. Then from that language they have been translated into other languages, such as Latin, Syriac, and others. The study of and instruction in the Irish language was not allowed, and, as was intended, it suffered a great loss in its cultural vocabulary. By this means they sought to drop all remembrance and to destroy all trace of the Bible origin and its authors. And this is why the Irish language was interdicted and forbidden to be taught in the schools, or even to be spoken. At one time, the British Government made it a crime punishable by death to speak it (McGeoghegan's *History of Ireland*). This makes it clear that the motive behind this policy was not, as hitherto advanced, solely a political one. But they found it convenient to retain the Irish idioms in the Bible for the name of God. It was difficult and next to impossible to find suitable substitutes in the translations for the ingenious and beautifully expressive titles of the Deity and of the Solar Sun in the Irish language. It is the richest language in spiritual expression that has yet been evolved in which to utter praise to God. Sanskrit and Hebrew are its children or offspring. Both of these languages were composed and given written form by the Irish (Aryan) missionary priesthood, but at very different periods. Hence, the similarity of these languages to the Irish.

Sanskrit was intended for the use of the priesthood which the Irish Missionaries established in India. It was changed, to suit the vocal peculiarities of the people whose use it was intended for, just enough from the parent (Irish) in phonetic and inflectional aspects. There can be no doubt about it. Here is what Max Muller says: "The Semitic languages also are all varieties of one form of speech. Though we do not know that primitive language from which the Semitic dialects diverged, yet we know. that at one time such language must have existed. . . . We cannot derive Hebrew from Sanskrit, or Sanskrit from Hebrew; but we can well understand how both may have proceeded from one common source. They are both channels supplied from one river, and they carry, though not always on the surface, floating materials of language which challenge comparison, and have already yielded satisfactory results to careful analyzers."

Max Muller's observations show that he was on the right path to discover the Mother Language of these two branches. All that he had to do was to look across the narrow sea which separates England from Ireland and find it there. Or did he not know that Irish was the "One River" which supplied both channels, and refrained from announcing it? He hits the nail so squarely on the head that it is hard to believe that so able and shrewd an investigator did not know. He was a professor of languages at Oxford, England, and well knew what an adverse sentiment would be aroused against him if he proclaimed it. He left it for another to do.

England had for so long a time stood between Ireland and the rest of the world that, after denuding her of her "ancient landmarks" and throwing a blanket of oblivion over her, he hesitated to remove it and be engulfed in the storm of wrath and enmity which he would arouse among the churchmen and the governing class of England. It is difficult for me to believe that so keen an observer was also, like so many other scholars and investigators, a credulous dupe, deluded by the false and perverted

histories of the past ages as written by the Roman and
British priest-scribes.   No, it is quite obvious that he
knew his England, and, if he wished to retain his profes-
sorship and standing he had to be careful as to what
extent he disclosed his discoveries and convictions. He
was treading on forbidden ground.

Hebrew was a secret dialect which was devised by the
Irish priesthood to preserve their secret lore and rituals.
Its use was kept exclusively for the priests, thereby
keeping all knowledge of sacerdotal things from the
uninitiated, or the laity.   As it was composed and made
use of by the Irish priests of Iesa to preserve their secret
lore, it was taken over and made use of by the Roman
Church to conceal and to make plausible the secret fraud
which she had perpetrated upon the Christian World.
This explains why it was said that only one copy of the
original first Scriptures was written in "Hebrew," and
this also shows us why Hebrew is so nearly like the Irish
language.   To further this deception she had them copied
into Greek.

This explains what has always been a puzzle to investigators, why the so-called Hebrew people who figured
in the myth with Jesus as his Apostles and who have
their own cultural Hebrew language should write the
four Gospels of the "New" Testament in Greek.

Hebrew was never spoken by the Aramaic people of
Syria, the so-called Jews, or by the people of any other
country.   It was used by the ancient Irish priesthood of
Iesa, precisely as Latin is today used in the Roman
Church to impress the multitude. The Roman priests

know this to be true, and many of the Protestant clergy know it and are conscious of being impostors and that they are perpetrating a cheat and a fraud which must be exposed for the scrutiny of the intellectual world of today.

In my studies and investigations in search of knowledge and light, I became convinced that Hebrew was an artificially constructed language of the priests, as in our day we have the newly constructed languages of Esperanto and Volupuk. I kept my discovery a secret, but in time I found that there were other investigators who had also discovered that Hebrew was not what the Roman and British churchmen have claimed it to be, that is, the national language of God's "chosen people" of a country in Asia — the Hebrew, or so-called Jewish race.

Here is what J. M. Pryse says:

"The Hebrew language was at first a secret sacerdotal jargon of Egyptian origin, and St. Gregory of Nyssa asserted (Oratio, p. 12) that the most learned men of his day knew positively that it was not as ancient as other languages, and did not become the spoken language of the Jews until after their departure from Egypt" (*The Apocalypse Unsealed*, p. 98).

The story of the Jews being captive in Egypt and later taking their departure from there is a pure myth, nicely constructed to deceive the unsophisticated, and represents the descent of the spirit of man into the flesh or body. The "Jew" represents the spirit, and Egypt, a cryptic name, represents the flesh or body. Egypt is a fabulous name formed for this purpose in the allegory.

The Irish brought religion and civilization to Egypt and that religion was Sun Worship. The word "Jew" is derived from an idiomatic Irish word Iudh (Yudh), meaning the day or light. It alludes to the Priests of the Sun, the followers of the Light, those who had wisdom. The word Iudh is camouflaged when it is converted into English by using the letter J instead of I to begin the word, there being no J in the Irish alphabet. So, by also leaving out the letters DH from the original Irish spelling, the "Doctors" have formulated the word "Jew." This deception being unsuspected, it has served the tricksters until now. There are other idiomatic names in the Irish language for "Jew" and "Hebrew" which give unmistakable proof that they are solely and truly of Irish origin. One of these names for "Jew" is Iuil (pronounced Yul). It expresses the attributes of the Sun when at His highest power and dignity, and is the name for the month Iuil (July). It is from this idea, which originated with and was developed by the Irish priests of Iesa, that was afterwards copied by the Roman church priests when they wrote their false history of Rome and bestowed the names of the months of the year, when the Sun is at his greatest power, upon two of their "historic" characters, Julius and Augustus Caesar. Iuil signifies, in Irish, learning, knowledge. The Irish attributed these qualities to the Sun, so, in accordance with this idea, the Roman priests, in their fictitious history, have Julius Caesar write a book. Thus we have a history of "Caesar's Campaigns," a priestly composition. These attributes were ascribed to the Sun by the

Irish Cult of Iesa, and those who embraced the religious life were the Jews, and not our "poor" brothers who own the City of New York.

A friend once told me that he had heard it stated that the Irish were the Hebrews. At the time, I thought the statement absurd and it made no impression. I took it more as a witticism or perhaps a cynical remark. But, to my own surprise, I have found that the statement was the real truth as regarding the ancient Irish.

It is very evident to me then that St. Gregory would make a play of exposing the "recent" origin of the Hebrew language if by so doing he could establish that it really ever was the language spoken by the fictitious "Jewish people" who were claimed to have been held as "captives" in historic Egypt. This is an example of how spurious authority has been set up by priest-scribes to make a fiction appear like fact, to make a false impression on the minds of men.

A recent writer in the public press made the statement that "the Irish language was spoken in the Garden of Eden," thereby implying that it was the God-given and original language of "Adam" and "Eve" and of the first patriarchs (Biblical Characters), and of the Master Adepts who wrote the first scriptures and formulated the mythical legend of our first parents, placing them in the "Garden of Eden." There is no doubt as to whom we are indebted for the Bible. It is the plainest and most evident truth, stripped of the disguise under which it has for so long a time been hidden by the British and Roman churchmen. Any scholar and thinker cannot fail to so recognize it, and many will blush to think that they did not see through it before.

The statement above quoted, regarding the Irish language, in the absence of correct knowledge, passed unnoticed, no doubt, by the general public, and, so far as I could see, brought no comment in the press. But to me, who had been engaged in research work in that line of study, it was full of significance. Whoever the writer may have been, he did not specify that it was the "Hebrew" language that was spoken by our "first parents," but, instead, the Irish language.

It would indeed be a strange phenomenon in the growth of language if two peoples of such different racial stocks, living so far apart in geographical location as Ireland and Syria, should speak the same, or nearly the same, language, and all the more so when it is a cultural language without there being a direct and special cause for it easy to understand. It is a self-evident impossibility.

The word Hebrew is derived from the Irish root word Ea (aodh, aoi), fire, the Vesta of the ancient Irish Priests of the Sun. The word in Irish is Eabhrach, which has been anglicized into Hebrew. Ea also signifies: a cause, matter in course of change, a compact, a confederacy, the learned, a vocation, learning, science, wise, a flock, knowledge, discipline, instruction, honor, respect, a country, an island, a tribe. This definition of the word Ea aptly applies to the cult of men which are meant to be secretly known by the term "Hebrew." So it is the name of a high order or degree of the ancient Irish Priests of the Sun, or the religion of Iesa Chriost, the

Sun God. They were the Priests of the Sacred Fire. So, from the roöt word Ea, we get the word Heber, meaning Fire, who is figuratively the "brother" of the Sun, and, hence, a Hebrew, the Priest of the Sun. All of which proves the Irish origin and character of the Hebrew Bible and its spiritual ideals and truths. It is this Irish evidence in the Bible which undoubtedly caused the idea to be advanced that the Irish were the "two lost tribes of Israel," which is but further evidence of "confusion worse confounded," as there never were two lost tribes in the sense set forth. It is purely mythical.

The following is a list of Irish words, which have been jargonized, with their "Hebrew" form. I might easily extend the list but this number of words will suffice to prove, as stated, that Hebrew is but a secret dialect reconstructed from the Irish for the use of the priesthood. Some words given here of both Irish and Hebrew are synonyms, others are slightly changed in meaning and form but plainly showing that they are of common origin. Such, for instance, are the Irish words Ciocras, pronounced Kucras, meaning hunger, and the word Cis, pronounced Kees, meaning rent. The Hebrew form of the first word is Chiceo, meaning "his palate"; and the second word has the same form as in the Irish and means a purse. Some words also have two or more forms, which are given.* This list makes it very

* In many Irish words there are dotted letters, which modifies the word; such letters have the aspirate letter h added. In such words the dotted letter becomes silent or modified, and the emphasis falls on the auxiliary letter, for example, the word Badaim, which, in form, becomes Badhaim (in the Irish the letter i is never dotted) and pro-

clear that a great deception has been practiced upon
the world.

IRISH	TRANSLATION	HEBREW
Ab	lord, master, abbot, father.	Ab
Abail	death.	Abad
Abailt	death.	Oved
Abu	war cry, death, sinking.	Aboi, Abaoi
Amna, Amhna	faithful, loyal.	Amunim
Aoir	a curse.	Arur
Asaire	shoemaker.	Asar
Ba	cows.	
Babun, Babhun	an inclosure for cattle, a town.	Bachon
Badaim, Badhaim	to drown, die, perish.	Abad
Baiste	showering, sprinkling, basting.	Bastek
Balb, Balbh	dumb, mute, inarticulate in utterance.	Balaim
Ban	woman, truth, light, white.	Bahin
Baogal, Baoghal	(pronounced Bahal) peril, danger.	Bahal
Baos	fornication, caprice, whim, frenzy, folly, wickedness.	Baash
Baot, Baoth	weak, soft, simple, frightened, terrified.	Baath
Bar	son.	Bar
Bar	learned man, scientific man, the sea, bread, food, a chief, the hair of the head.	Barah
Baran	a baron, food bread.	Barah
Bas	death.	Bus

nounced Bahaim. To assist those who may not be acquainted with this
feature of the Irish alphabet, I have added to such words their modified
form, which accounts for the second word in the Irish list.

Irish	Translation	Hebrew
Basaim	to put to death.	Bus
Basgaim	to stop or stay, check, drown, oppress, trample.	Bus
Bat, Bata	a stick, staff, pole, branch.	Bad
Bath, Both	hut, tent, house.	Beth
Bath, Bathadh	(t and d silent) destruction, drowning.	Bahah
Batal, Bathal	danger.	Ballahah, Behalah
Beice	clamorous weeping.	Bechi, Beche, Bechith
Biag, Biagh	food.	Bag
Bile	a mouth, lip, border, a welt, a large tree, a cluster of trees.	Bul
Biordan, Biordan	calumny, falsehood.	Bies
Bior	pin, bodkin.	Beriach
Biorac, Biorach	sharp-pointed.	Beriach
Biseac, Biseach, Biseacht	prosperity, increase, profit, gain.	Bizza, Baz
Boc, Phic	he-goat, deceit, fraud.	Phuch, Phich
Boċd, Bochd	poor, needy, miserable, distressed, lean, meager.	Boka
Bogadac, Bogadach	gesture, rocking, unstable.	Bagheda
Bruighean	palace, royal residence.	Birah
Buacais	wick of a candle, confusion.	Buch
Caem, Caemh	feast, love, desire.	Cama
Cail	desire, strength, valor, the back.	Chail
Cailliac, Cailliach	old woman.	Calach
Caisc	the feast of Easter.	Pasch
Caite	winnowed, a bruise, wound.	Chathe
Calb, Calbh	hardness, bald, baldpated.	Chalak

IRISH	TRANSLATION	HEBREW
Cam	quarrel, deceit, injustice, crooked.	Camak
Caoin	gentle, mild, sweet-tempered, kind, clement.	Chen
Caoirig, Cro	sheepfold.	Ceroth
Caoradh	furnace, sheep.	Cur
Carrac, Carrach	scabbed, mangy, bald.	Karrach
Cas	plague, money, fear, anxiety, difficulty, hasty, passionate, sudden.	Chush
Casog	coat, garment, cassock, cloak, covering.	Casa, Cisa
Catair, Cathair	(pronounced Cahir) city, ward, cathedral.	Kariah, Kiriah
Catal, Cathal	valor.	Cail
Cead-tus, Cead-thus	an element, beginning.	Cadish
Ceal	covering, concealing, death, heaven, forgetfulness, use, fine flour, sickness.	Coli
Cealad, Cealadh	eating, consuming.	Cilla
Ceile	spouse, husband or wife, companion, associate.	Calla
Ceim	step, degree, elevation, dignity.	Cum
Ci, Cia	who, what, how.	Ci
Ciocras	hunger, greediness, longing, covetousness.	Chiceo
Cis	rent.	Cis
Cleas	play, frolic, prank, feat, trick, sham, craft, dexterity.	Cheles
Clum, Clumh	feather, down, plume, fur, hair.	Chloim
Collaim	I sleep.	Cholom

IRISH	TRANSLATION	HEBREW
Creapad, Crea-padh	contraction.	Charp
Crios	belt, girdle, band, the Sun.	Cheres
Cupa, Cupan	cup.	Gabiong
Curud, Curudh	banquet.	Cora
Dag	fish.	Daga
Daid	father	Dod
Dirig, Diric	to direct.	Derech, Derach
Dìbead, Dibeadh	daubing, slandering.	Dibba
Did	pap, dug.	Dad
Dob	plaster, gutter, mire.	Dob
Dub, Dubh	great, prodigious, black, burned.	Dobhe
Dubacas, Dub-hachas	sadness, sorrow.	Dove
Duille, Duilleog	leaf of a tree or book, fold, sheath, scabbard.	Aleh
Duineabhadh	manslaughter, mortality.	Bath, Batha
Eas	cataract, waterfall, cascade.	Eshed
Eilid, Eilidh	a hind.	Aceleth
Eis	a man.	Aish
Epeac, Epeach	strong, vehement.	Aphic
Er	great, noble, good.	Ereel
Esdor	halter.	Ezor
Fadaim	I expound, explain.	Fatsa
Faosad, Faosadh	collecting.	Pasadh
Gadaide, Ga-daidhe	thief.	Gadud
Gail	smoke, vapor, fume, steam, slaughter, valor, virtue.	Chail
Gamal	fool, stupid person.	Gamal
Gaot, Gaoth	dart, stitch, shooting pain, theft, the sea, the wind.	Gaah, Gaha

Irish	Translation	Hebrew
Garb, Garbh	scab, scabbiness, warfare, courage.	Garab
Gas	bunch, stalk, stem or bough of a plant, young boy, military servant, anger, indignation.	Geze
Ger	ruminating.	Gerah
Gle, Glee	rejoicing, pure, clean, open, plain, discovered, good, perfect, enough, sufficiency.	Gul
Gob	mouth, beak, snout.	Gab
Grib	dirt, slough.	Regeb
Iall	shoe.	Naal
Iall	flock, herd, drove, latchet, thong.	Naal
Iarsma	relic, remnant.	Iaresh, Iaresha
Iarsmac, Iarsmach	beneficent, generous.	
Iarsmact, Iarsmacht	generosity, bounty.	
Iomaire	a ridge.	Amir
Iosact, Iosacht	a loan.	Jashe
Iosa	(Jesus.)	Jehoshuah
Lamac, Lamhach	(pronounced Lamah) having hands, active, playing with, handling, shooting, slugging, casting.	Lamah
Saindrean	seat, society, sect.	Sanhedrim
Sam, Samh	pleasant, still, calm, tranquil.	Samah
Sac	sack, bag.	Sak
Saoth	life, existence, prince.	Seet
Scian	knife.	Sakin
Sciobol	barn, granary.	Schibol
Se	he, it, him.	Se
Sealg	a chase, hunting.	Shalach

Irish	Translation	Hebrew
Sean	ancestor, old, ancient.	Iashan
Seisir, Seisreach	six persons or things, a plow of six horses.	Asar, Eisir
Sgaoll	fear, shyness, fright.	Sakal
Sileadh	a dropping, twinkling of the eyes.	Zillel
Sion	phenomenon, brightness, Heaven.	Zion
Suibhal	going, moving, walking.	Shubh
Suiblach	a traveler.	Shebhila
So	this, this here, this is.	So
Sochar	gain, profit, prosperity.	Sacar
Sopog	wisp of straw or hay.	Sapach
Suan	sleep, deep sleep.	Shena
Tacar	plenty, gleaning, provision.	Dagar
Tula	hill, hillock.	Tel
Tumba	tomb, grave.	Dum
Ur	fresh, new earth, the Sun, a man, a heath.	Ur

Every Celtic scholar, investigator and thinker will at once comprehend the incontrovertible nature of the proof here submitted in this list of Irish words with their Hebrew derivatives as to who the "Jews" and "Hebrews" were. British and Roman lies cannot prevail against it.

The ancient Irish priesthood of Iesa had not only a secret system of writing called "Ogham," but they had also special dialects formulated from the Irish language, each being a perfect language in itself, such as for Law, Music, etc. One of these dialects was our so-called Hebrew language which was reserved exclusively for the use of the priests. It was used for ritualistic purposes and to secretly preserve their spiritual ideals. It was made use of by the Roman Church after the suppression of the Irish Church. From this list of words it can be seen that the "Hebrew" words are just altered and changed enough from the original to deceive the unsuspecting among the Irish laity, who by chance might happen to have access to it. But to the non-Irish of a later day, or people of other races, it could easily be made to appear as an original language developed by a distinctly different race of people said to be called Hebrew.

So, by means of suppressing the cultural Irish language it was easy for Rome, with the aid of her British confederates, to easily enough palm off on the world the "Hebrew" Bible. It was translated into Greek in accordance with the plan for concealment and for the purpose of staging the drama of the Bible Story and episodes over in Palestine. It has been transcribed and altered many times since, but even yet its "ancient landmarks" are still there. The people who settled these American Colonies knew nothing of the fraud that was perpetrated on them regarding the scriptures, and they have unwittingly passed on the deception to the people of our day. With the aid of the art of printing and the zeal of creed propaganda, the deception has spread among the ignorant masses as well as among the so-called enlightened, with the exception of the Roman and English clergy. No impartial student can study the Irish language without becoming convinced that it is the original language of the scriptures. Ample proof of this fact will be found all through these pages and even in the short list of Irish and Hebrew words which has been submitted here. The Irish Roman Catholic priests, who have been the custodians of the literary language, have been guilty of deletion. And it is evident that in the compilation of Irish dictionaries there are many omissions of words, a thing not to be wondered at when the purpose behind such omission is known. However, there is sufficient evidence left to prove the Bible to be of unmistakable Irish origin, without a shadow of doubt, and also to furnish convincing evidence that the ancient Irish were the so-called "Chosen People" of the Bible story. The man who was striving to live a spiritual life was an Iudach (Jew), from Iudh (the day), showing that he was a disciple or a devotee of the Sun. Those who had advanced and were seeking a higher order of spirituality are, in the Bible story, called the Israelites or disciples of Iesa, the God of the Sun, and His spirit in man. The average man or the common run of humanity is comprehended in the term "Philistine." This word is taken from the Irish word Fuil, pronounced fihl, meaning blood. It also signifies a family or tribe. In its Biblical application it comprehends all those who are absorbed in carnal things, the flesh and the world, rather than the things of the spirit, so meaning the "worldly ones."

With this revelation of truth we can see readily why the assembly of clerics, who revised the Bible from time to time, always did so behind closed and barred doors. They were put under oath not to reveal the matters which were discussed while that work was being done, a conspiracy to suppress and hide the truth from the people. We must consider that Christian theology is taken bodily from the ancient Irish concept of the Beneficent and Creative Sun, for a center and ideal, and disguised so that it could not be traced. Recognizing that fact, a knowledge of the Irish language will enable any investigator to recognize the original parent language of the Bible. The great injustice done to the Irish people and to the so-called Jews of our day becomes at once apparent.

The theological idea of the ancient Irish priesthood was that the Sun was the Logos, the Creator, and greatest representative of God. It was through the Sun that all good came to mankind. The Sun was The Great Being through whom was received light and knowledge. All good came through the Sun and He was the greatest visible representative of The Great Unseen Deity. Any man among the Irish who was ready to enter the search for light, the spiritual life, was known as an Iudach (Jew) and entered into the path of the spiritual life. The Sun was the embodiment of all that was good, and the Irish personified Him as a champion, warrior, and hero whom they strove to emulate.

There is no mistaking the ideals and idiomatic names in the Irish language, the first cultural language, on this point, as the following words will show.

From the word Iudh (day) we get Iudach (pronounced Yudach), Iudaigheach, and Iuduighe, three different forms to express the name Jew, which stood for the followers of the Day or Sun. And the Irish word

Iudiceacht, judgment, is from the same root. These words are not borrowed words engrafted on the language, but are of the parent stem. Another name of "Jew" deep rooted in the Irish language, and all the sophistry in Roman or English High Churchdom cannot remove it, is Iuil, pronounced Yul, a Jew. Why does this happen to be so? It is because with the ancient Irish priesthood of The Sun, the embodiment of all good, He was in his highest power and potency after "climbing the hill" (up to the Sun's day — the 24th of June) during the month of Iuil (July). He manifested Himself in warm sunshiny days, dispensing His beneficence to all nature and to mankind. These warm days were, metaphorically speaking, called His "companions," and, therefore, were said to be his "disciples." The month of Iul was the month of His essential power and warmth, and from that fact His initiated devotee of the priesthood of Iesa was called an Iuil (Jew) after the Sun's aspect and attributes.

As the Sun is the visible center of light, He is the great teacher. He contains and imparts to mankind all light and knowledge. All who are wise in esoteric things recognize this to be true. As to His natural aspect in relation to the physical world, His beneficence and influence are everywhere manifested. All earthly life depends upon the Sun.

The Irish word Iul signifies knowledge, learning, art, science, judgment, a way, attendance, light, the month Iul and Iuil, a Jew. From the same root we get the words Iulaidhe, a leader; Iullagach, sprightly, light,

cheerful; Iulmhar, wise, judicious; Iulmharach, skill-
ful. These facts and the lesson of truth they convey
can be verified by anyone who will investigate.

The Duke of Argyll (the *Unity of Nature*) says: "We
have found in the most ancient records of the Aryan
language proof that the indications of religious thought
are higher, simpler and purer as we go back in time."
(Quoted in Donnelly's *Atlantis*, p. 447.)

We have taken our readers back to the etymological
foundation of the word "Jew." It is of the very warp
and woof of the first cultural language that was spoken
in this round of existence, the language evolved by the
Great Magian Priests of Eire, during thousands of years
before their migration towards the East, to give light and
knowledge to the younger and undeveloped races of
mankind.

CHAPTER XI

THE IRISH THE FIRST CULTURAL NATION, THE EARLIEST MISSIONARY TEACHERS, AND THE GREAT TEMPLE BUILDERS OF THE ANCIENT WORLD

ONE of the aims of the propaganda for spreading misinformation regarding Ireland was to create an impression, because of a similarity between the customs of the Irish and those of the Hindoos, that the Irish and their customs came originally from the East, or India. Really, on the contrary, this fact only confirms the truth that the Irish gave their customs to the Hindoos during their missionary sojourn in that country. The Hindoos have never been known as a colonizing race, while we have overwhelming evidence to show that Ireland was the greatest colonizing country of the ancient world. They were the real pathfinders of the world. As to the likelihood of a Hindoo migration to Ireland in the past, the author of *Atlantis* says (p. 416) : "The Hindoos have never within the knowledge of man sent out colonies or fleets for exploration; but there is abundant evidence, on the other hand, of migrations from Atlantis * eastward." "And how," he asks, "could the Sanskrit writings have preserved maps of Ireland, England, and Spain, giving the shape and outline of their coasts, and

* Atlantis is but a fictitious name for Ireland. — C. M. D.

161

their very names, and yet have preserved no memory
of the expeditions or colonizations by which they acquired
that knowledge?"   Once the plain truth is made known,
the plot of the conspirators becomes evident on all sides,
and the fabricators of spurious history are seen to have
gone to such absurd lengths, among others, as to invent
the fabulous tale of the "lost continent of Atlantis,"
described by "Plato," in order to carry out their purpose
to obscure Ireland's great past.   This great past, if
known, would at once prove to the whole world that
Ireland was the original parent country of learning, the
sciences, and spiritual culture, and the Motherland of
true religion.   This fact is cryptically preserved by
tradition and the myth that schools were established there
by Ollom Ollo, which name means Doctor or Professor
of Science, and indicates the High Hierophant of the
Irish Magian Sun Cult.   It is also alluded to in the story
of "Cadmus" (first one), the first to establish schools.
It is further confirmed by the tradition, veiled in cryptic
form, that long before real or actual schools were established there, a certain Phineas Pharsa (from Phin,
The Sun, and Phar, a man, — a Finician) had established
schools on the plains of "Shinar" (us, we, ourselves).
This fabled place, for the purpose of deception, has been
located in Persia.   This "Phineas Pharsa" and the
"plains of Shinar" is but a secret allusion to the fact
that the Irish Magian Adept Cult of The Sun Worship,
who here on this island were the first men to develop the
latent or potential intellectual and spiritual powers
within themselves, here erected the first schools and laid

the foundation for all the culture, religious and secular, which exists in the world today.   This is a fact of fundamental truth, which nothing can shake or destroy. It is attested to on all sides, upon close examination, by the cultural idioms of the Bible and the esoteric truths preserved in the symbolic monuments of The Great Pyramid Group in Egypt and elsewhere in the East. They have left indisputable evidence of this culture in the religious rites and institutions which they introduced here when they brought Sun Worship and civilization to both North and South America.   There is the most incontestable proof of this, as will be shown later on.

This purpose to obscure a knowledge of her history and institutions may be further seen in the effort which has been made to create a doubt as to the origin of her round towers and the purpose for which they were erected. There is no doubt whatever, in the writer's mind, but that the Round Tower has always been a *stubborn* fact for them to dispose of, and we are not surprised to find that they have *on hand* records (fabricated since the invasion) which will show that many of those towers were destroyed by an act of nature instead of by the willful acts of ruthless destroyers.   One of the methods employed by those fabricators to isolate and minimize Ireland's historical importance is pretty well reflected, as will be noted, in the description given by "Diodorus Siculus," intended for effect on posterity, portraying her as some obscure and little-known island in some remote and unfrequented part of the Atlantic Ocean. Just as if he were introducing a knowledge of her to the world for the first time, or preserving her very name from oblivion. The excerpt which will show this implied mendacity on the part of "Diodorus" will also include as an authority the untruthful Geraldus Cambrinsis. In referring to the latter, Mr. Donnelly is evidently not aware of his untruthful character. So we find him again, among others, in his rôle as an "authority," as was intended. Regarding the Round Towers, those unique and peculiarly original Irish monuments connected with Sun Worship, Mr. Donnelly says: "Attempts have been made to show, by Dr. Petrie and others, that these extraordinary structures are of modern origin, and were built by the Christian priests, in which to keep their church-plate. But it is shown that the 'Annals of Ulster' mention the destruction of fifty-seven of them by an earthquake in A.D. 448; and Geraldus Cambrinsis shows that Lough Neagh was created by an inundation, or sinking of the land, in A.D. 65. . . ." Moreover, we find Diodorus Siculus, in a well-known passage, referring to Ireland, and describing it as "an island in the ocean over against Gaul, to the North, and not inferior in size to Sicily, the soil of which is so fruitful that they mow there twice in the year." Donnelly goes on to say: "He mentions the skill of their harpers, their sacred groves, *and their singular temples of round form*" (*Atlantis*, pp. 416–17).

We here see a conflict of opinion in the statements attributed to "Dr. Petrie and others" and "Diodorus Siculus." We are reminded of a proverb which says: "A lie must have long legs or it will be overtaken." The propagandists have evidently suffered a lapse of memory right here on this point, regarding the antiquity of those towers.

The effect of all this false information has been to set men astray in their quest for a solution as to what country or people we are indebted to for those monuments.   Sir John Lubbock (quoted in *Atlantis*, p. 417) says : "They have been supposed by some to be Scandinavian, but no similar buildings exist in Norway, Sweden, or Denmark, so that this style of architecture is no doubt anterior to the arrival of the Northmen." (That is, their arrival in Ireland.)

It seems puerile and absurd that any investigator possessing even the ordinary amount of acumen necessary to deal with the subject of the Round Towers should honestly think, much less circulate the opinion, that the towers were built in Roman Christian times, and give as a reason that it was a place where the priests kept their church-plate.   It is, to say the least, disingenuous.   The knowledge necessary to the solution of the question of the Round Towers is not obscure or remote from men who, even in a small measure, have given thought to the investigation of things symbolic.   The explanation of the Round Tower is simple, and the purpose of its use easy to apprehend.   This understanding will at once enable anyone to determine in what country it originated and who the builders were.   Those who are responsible for disseminating misinformation know this fact well; the misinformation is but a part of the plan of concealment.

The Round Tower is peculiarly an Irish or Aryan

symbol of the Sun Worship. In their world-wide migrations to preach the Gospel the Irish erected the towers in association with their Temples. They are symbols of the phallus, and represent the creative power of God, through the Lord Sun Iesa, both in Nature and in Man. It has a natural, mystical, and spiritual significance. The same idea has been borrowed and embodied in the modern church spire. The remains of those towers are found as far apart from Ireland as India, in the East, and from Ireland to New Mexico and Colorado, in the West. The author of *Atlantis* (p. 418) most pertinently says: "It will not do to say that the resemblance between these prehistoric and singular towers, in countries so far apart as Sardinia, Ireland, Colorado, and India, is due to an accidental coincidence."

It is sometimes necessary in dealing with a shameless and persistent propaganda of falsehood to speak in a plain and direct manner, especially against powerful and subtle agencies which have been able, through means of the written page as a medium for misrepresentation, either by alteration or by omission altogether, so successfully to obliterate and reduce to an unimportant and insignificant character the history, or story, of the greatest nation of ancient times, if not of all time. The commercial greatness of this nation was unrivaled; her universities and schools of learning, not only in mediæval times but anciently, made her the "Intellectual Sun of Europe," as Professor Sigerson of Dublin recently declared. Without any exaggeration whatever, and with justice, we may supplement his statement and say that she was truly the intellectual light of the whole world. Her ethical culture has never been equaled, let alone surpassed, as evidenced by our Bible, which, when rightly understood, with its ideal counterpart in stone — The Great Pyramid Temple Pillar of Iesa — is her crowning glory. So it becomes very apparent why there has been such an amount of feigned ignorance regarding the origin of the Round Towers and the failure of those with knowledge to give out correct information about them. It is absolutely certain and without a shadow of doubt that the Papal Hierarchy at Rome, and its members in Britain and Ireland as well, were in possession of this knowledge, and that they also had a lively knowledge of the long and continuous intercourse between Ireland and the American Continent, or Land of the West. The traditions of this intercourse never died out among the Irish. The old tradition of "St. Brendan" sailing to the "Land of the West" in A.D. 545 * from the foot of the great headland in Kerry which bears his name is but

* Dates are unreliable. "There are eleven Latin MSS. in the Bibliothéque Impériale at Paris of this legend, the dates of which vary from the eleventh to the fourteenth century, but all of them anterior to the time of Columbus" (*Atlantis*, p. 240). These dates are evidently fictitious and spurious, and are, we believe, intended to provide "authentic records" that would show, in case of need, that St. Brendan's voyage was a rare and unusual one and made close to the time of the jurisdiction of the Romish Church rule in Ireland, which, as stated, began in the 12th century. But the alleged date of 545 A.D., which is given as the date of the voyage, even brings it within the time in which the Irish are supposed to have been converted to Christianity by "St. Patrick." These dates are intended as an alibi by which to explain any resemblance which might be discovered later between ancient American religious rites and institutions and those of Roman Christianity.

merely a ray to shed light upon this fact. There is evidence that the fact of this intercourse was a common tradition along the Atlantic Coast of Europe; and it is safe to say that Rome knew of the colonizations made by the Irish on the Western Continent and of the religious establishments which it was their wont to set up wherever they planted a colony. With due caution to the reader to make a proper allowance for the attempt of the Roman Churchman always to connect the Irish with the Roman Church, we will let the Abbé Brasseur de Bourbourg speak on this point. In a note to his translation of the sacred book of the Mayas, the "Popol Vuh" (quoted in *Atlantis*, p. 419), he says: "There is an abundance of legends and traditions concerning the passage of the Irish into America, and their habitual communication with that continent many centuries before the time of Columbus. We should bear in mind that Ireland was colonized by the Phoenicians (or by people of that race). An Irish Saint named Vigile, who lived in the eighth century, was accused to Pope Zachary of having taught heresies on the subject of the Antipodes. At first he wrote to the Pope in reply to the charge, but afterward he went to Rome in person to justify himself, and there he proved to the Pope that the Irish had been accustomed to communicate with a transatlantic world." *

* It may easily be seen from this evidence that, although this Irish Saint is given a Latin name, he was teaching a theory and pursuing a course which was deemed a heresy by the *Roman Church Fathers*, and it is the strongest presumptive evidence that the Irish Church was independent of Rome at that time. If he had been a member of the Roman Church, he would not have dared to preach such open heresy;

In view of the knowledge which we possess today and the belief which is founded upon that knowledge, it is worth while to consider here, if but briefly, some of the circumstances connected with the voyage of Columbus. In the accounts, be it remembered, we have been informed that he sought aid from the Church Fathers. He traveled about from one church establishment to another, and it is said that he went to Rome to seek aid there. However that may be, a junta composed mostly of the Church Fathers in Spain, after hearing his views and beliefs, refused him assistance or approval. This opposition lasted for a number of years, but was later evidently withdrawn, as we find that it was through the influence of a Father Confessor of a Spanish monastery that King Ferdinand and Queen Isabella fitted out the expedition which enabled Columbus to embark upon the voyage westward. Spain at the time, with its King and Queen, was almost completely under the Church influence. We are told that Columbus's reason for embarking on this voyage was an ardent desire to plant the standard of the Cross in the new lands which he might discover and that he believed that by sailing westward he would be able to find a new trade route to the Indies. These reasons which have been given out are specious and may be dismissed as not being the true

and neither would he have had an option as to whether or not he would have gone to Rome. He would have been peremptorily summoned there for his heresy and disciplined. The very fact of his voluntary appearance there proves his independence, regardless of his facts. At the time stated there were yet many Irish monks and scholars belonging to the Irish Church on the European Continent.

motives. As for the desire to set up the Cross, — we
will see that this expedition and subsequent ones, under
the leadership of the priests, destroyed the Cross wherever they found it on this Western Hemisphere. And we
may also set aside as fiction the fitting out of the expedition to discover a new trade route to the East because
the Turks or Moslems dominated the overland trade
route to that part of the world. In the absence of
knowledge, this latter reason has appeared plausible.
In order to sustain this impression as to the object of the
voyage, we are told that the two commercial and trading
republics of Venice and Genoa suffered most by the loss
of the eastern trade route and that they were especially
clamorous for the discovery of a new route to the East.
Now, if this were a fact, why did not these two states,
each comprising a seafaring people equipped with
fleets and eager for commerce and trade, send their
fleets to the West to trade and make discoveries after the
news of Columbus's successful voyage had spread abroad?
They were the two greatest maritime states in the
Mediterranean, if not in Europe, at that time. If they
needed a trade route so badly, would they not have
entered into competition with the other nations for their
share of the trade and spoils? Instead of those two
states, whom we have been told wanted it most, we find
Spain, Portugal, England, France, and Holland monop-
olizing the trade and the spoils of discovery. None of
these nations were better equipped for overseas trade
or voyages than Venice and Genoa, and it is rather surprising that the latter did not engage in the western

trade. If their need were so great, would not the Pope, when he assumed to divide the New World into spheres, allotting one to Spain and another to Portugal, be very likely to assign spheres respectively to those two Italian City States? The whole thing is merely a part of the fabric of lies invented to conceal the real motive for projecting the voyage. Columbus was said to have been a Genoese, but discoveries have been made since which show that he was a Spanish subject, born and bred in Spain. Thus, it is obvious that the alleged reasons for the voyage are false and will not do. They have been accepted heretofore without close examination.

There was another and far more urgent reason for the voyage. But, before proceeding to give the real cause back of it, let us dispose of the excuse of the Turkish or Moslem menace to commerce between Europe and the East, which was but dust for the eyes so that men would not be able to see the real motive. There had been constant commerce carried on between the West and East, not only during the period of time we are dealing with, but long before and since over the land and sea route from the Mediterranean, through Constantinople, and by devious routes eastward. The Moslems have dominated the main eastern overland route for more than seven hundred years. There was a partial interruption to their sway during the Crusades when the Christians held the Kingdom of Jerusalem for a period of eighty-eight years. This kingdom fell in 1187 A.D., and the period of the Crusades came to an end about 1285 A.D. It was not the Turk who stood in the way of commerce or trade as such. The Crusades were brought on by Rome, who instigated the Christian nations of Europe to attack the Moslems in order that she might possess the so-called Holy Land. The Turks were forced to defend themselves and the land which had been in their hands for some centuries. But there was no unsurmountable barrier to peace if Rome had wished peace, when again the stream of commerce could have resumed its wonted flow. The Turks have never abjured trade or commerce. During the wars of the Crusades, the most frightful massacres and excesses were committed, due to Christian fanaticism. Yet, despite all this, the Moslem King Saladin of Egypt and the Greek Emperor Alexius of Byzantium had no difficulty in coming to a mutual understanding and making peace between themselves and the peoples of their respective countries. But with the Roman Church it was different. The Fatimite Caliph of Egypt wanted to make peace with the Roman Church cohorts, and he "offered to guarantee to all unarmed pilgrims an unmolested sojourn of one month in Jerusalem, and to aid the Crusaders on their march to the Holy City, if they would acknowledge his supremacy within the bounds of his Syrian Empire" (*Enc. Brit.*, 9th Ed., p. 625). His proposal for peace was rejected. Rome was out for spoils and possessions to increase her income and power. The onus belongs to Rome for whatever of interruption there was to commerce with the East, and this could have been removed at any time, we believe, if Rome had earnestly desired it. It can readily be seen that the demand for a new trade route could not have been very strong or Rome would have had to yield to it. So we may dismiss this reason as an invention. Moreover, if a new trade route was to be found, why look to the westward for it? We have been taught to believe, through interested sources, that the western ocean, in the time of Columbus, was believed to be an unknown and limitless waste of waters holding the most forbidding and frightful terrors and peopled by hideous monsters of gruesome shapes who would destroy anyone venturesome enough to attempt to go far to the westward. After the conquest and absorption of the Irish Church, such fictions may have been spread among the masses by the Roman Church priests, and in a few generations they would have found a wide belief. If so, they served a purpose for Rome for the time being, while she was consolidating her conquests in different parts, and strengthening her organization for future expansion and growth. The astute leaders of the church held no such notions regarding the western ocean. The mental medicine they prescribe for the multitude is something apart, and always has been, from what they themselves partake of. So, on that point there is not the least room for doubt; for, if they believed such silly fiction, it is only reasonable to suppose that they would not have at any time favored the project. That the voyage had another objective than that given out by the priests, we may well believe. The circumstances under which the voyage was promoted and aided merits a much more extended elucidation than I am privileged, from the nature of this work, to give here.

Let me briefly call attention to the struggle in which

Ferdinand and Isabella were engaged with the Moors in an endeavor to reclaim the Kingdom of Granada. The completion of this struggle left the King and Queen as exhausted of all means as did the Crusades leave practically all Europe. And more especially did the Fathers of the Church feel the effects due to the Crusades in the loss of revenue from properties and privileges which they had formerly held but which were now taken over by the Kings and nobility to recoup, in a measure, the losses sustained in those wars to advance the interests of the church organization. This state of affairs had a direct bearing on the project of Columbus's voyage and on the final decision to promote it. The resources of Ferdinand and Isabella were so low that she had to pledge her jewels in order to find the means to furnish the necessary vessels and supplies.

The War against the Moors which reduced Spain to such an extremity was waged, in a measure, as much in behalf of the Church — to banish the infidel and reclaim the country for Christendom — as it was to regain the country for the Crown of Spain. The country, as a consequence, was in a terrible state of poverty, and the Church was also financially lean. This state of affairs, coupled with the fear that, owing to the persistence of Columbus in seeking aid which might be granted by some one whom the Church could not control, caused them, after due deliberation, to promote the voyage at that particular time.

That the Papal authorities at Rome had long possessed a pretty good knowledge of the Irish intercourse with the

Western Continent we may well believe; this knowledge they obtained from the Irish priests as stated by the Abbé Brasseur de Bourbourg. In fact, it would have been next to impossible to have kept this knowledge from them, as Ireland was the greatest maritime nation in the world and *the one* with which Rome had the longest struggle we have any record or tradition of. So it goes without saying that the hierarchy at Rome knew that the Irish Church of Iesa Chriost had established Christianity, or Sun Worship, on the Western Continent. This knowledge must have been confirmed by the Irish priests who were brought into the Roman Church organization at the time of the suppression of the Irish Church.

So, when the project of the western voyage was first proposed, it was looked upon with ill favor by the Church Fathers, because they considered it inopportune and the time inauspicious. They feared that the voyage would lead to the discovery and revelation of facts before the whole world which would be damaging to the Church. Therefore, they tried to dissuade Columbus, under various pretexts and discouragements, to give up the idea, and in every manner possible, by argument, ridicule, and false logic, to convince him that he held erroneous ideas concerning the shape of the earth. By a display of "superior learning" they sought to convince him that his theory and beliefs were alike fallacious. In the light of what transpired, it seems that those men, when they found that they could not dissuade Columbus from his purpose, parried for delay, and, in the meantime, they formulated a plan of policy by which they could prevent intelligence of any damaging facts, which might be discovered, from spreading abroad. It was only after this decision was made, we believe, that enough information about the Western Continent and the great wealth which existed there was made known privily to Ferdinand and Isabella. And it was this information which decided her to sell her jewels, her very last available assets, to finance the expedition. Considering the war in which the royal pair were then engaged and the sacrifices which they had already made to advance the interests of the Church, it is not reasonable to suppose that the priests would have encouraged or advised her to part with her jewels, her last penny, to back a wild and foolish proposition, as they had hitherto held it to be. But they now gave both her and the King assurances that the outcome of the voyage was a certainty beyond merely the ordinary hazards of the sea.

In view of the knowledge in our possession, a fact may be stated here, and one of no little importance in this connection; and that is that a companion of Columbus on this voyage is listed on the rolls as "William, the Irishman, from Dublin." In view of the importance which attached to this enterprise, and what was openly staked upon it by his royal patron and secretly expected of it by the Church Fathers, it is but natural to suppose that men of the best nautical skill and knowledge were secured to assist Columbus. So it is only fair to assume that this person was sea-wise in the knowledge of the Irish mariners, who were formerly the unrivaled sea voyagers of the world, from time out of mind, their

nearest competitors, but far inferior in range, being the
Norse of a later day.   This Irishman William may have
previously made such a voyage himself, which might
account for his being with Columbus on this voyage.   If
such was the case, no record of it would have been allowed
to exist.   The systematic suppression of facts, which is
almost beyond belief, of the history of Irish achievements,
is most shameless and barefaced, carried on by agencies
already mentioned.   It is the plainest fact that Ireland's
history has been written by her enemies.   However, it is
important to note that an Irishman was one of the
personnel of that voyage.   He was of the race of seamen
who made voyages across the western ocean and had a
constant intercourse with the people of this American
Continent from the time of the Bronze Age (See *Atlantis*,
Art. "Bronze Age in Europe," pp. 237, 238, 246, 249, 259,
260, 266, 267).   It is a fair conjecture, to say the least,
that he brought some particular and special knowledge
to Columbus and was familiar with the seafaring traditions of his race.

The Church Fathers, in all essentials, practically
ruled the Spanish Kingdom and were the closest advisers
of the King and Queen.   Those shrewd men, crafty
strategists, with a world perspective for their organization, knew of the Irish Church colonization on the
opposite side of the Atlantic; and that it was from there
that the priests of the Irish Church obtained the gold and
silver for their church service and for the ornaments of
their symbolic monuments, Pyramids, Temples, Towers,
Obelisks, and Dallans.   Ireland itself, so far as known,

never yielded more than a small amount of those metals, and they were dedicated to the use of the Sun Worship. The policy decided upon, judging by what actually occurred, was to place a close censorship upon the voyage. The same policy was applied to subsequent voyages, and all along we find the priest accompanying every voyage and in the van of every expedition.

He was there to observe everything discovered and to bring back a report to his superiors, and, more especially, to take note of the religious state and conditions which were found existing in the Western Land. He was there also for the purpose of mutilating and destroying whatever evidence might be found that would be injurious or damaging to the claims of the Roman Church. This evidence was found in abundance everywhere, as will be shown.

All things considered, there is no other hypothesis but this outstanding fact upon which to account for the sack and ruin of temples and altars, monuments and symbols, as well as the destruction of cities, coupled with the awful killings and massacres committed by the Spaniards, dominated by the priests, upon a highly civilized, peaceable, and practically unarmed people. They received the Spaniards as friends, even as the traditional "fair Gods" (bearded white men), the Irish Magi, returning to them again, as was expected and promised, — they received them with open hospitality and welcome. The recompense they received in turn was frightful and savage. They were slaughtered, with the result that in a few short years the population was reduced in numbers, their leaders killed off, their civilization destroyed, and their temples and religious institutions ruined. This happened not only in Mexico, but also in Yucatan and Peru. It is not my purpose to go into this phase of Spanish policy extensively here, much less to treat of the enslavement of the natives; but only to show the underlying motive that was back of such action on the part of the Spaniards. This will be seen by what the priests discovered.

They found here, as was expected, an abundance of proof of the Irish or Aryan connection with the religious institutions in Mexico, Peru, and elsewhere on this American Continent. They were practically the same in both North and South America. It was the Irish Sun Worship or Christianity which prevailed among the civilized inhabitants of both continents. The name Cuzco, the Capital of Peru, the Seat of the Sun Worship in South America, testifies to their establishing a colony there. For Cuzco is an Irish Name of the Sun God (from Cais, meaning an eye, haste, a twist or turn — whirling — a stream, love, virility, — of the Sun in Spring). The Sun God Casga is still worshiped to this day, not only in Ireland, but throughout the entire Christian world, on "Domhnaig Casga" (Easter Sunday), the day of the Risen Sun in Springtime. The City of Cuzco was the Seat of the Ainca (Inca) or head of the Sun Worship in the Southern Continent. These facts alone, even in the absence of other direct, positive, and indisputable proof, should leave no doubt whatever as to who discovered and civilized ancient America.

I will briefly mention some only of the rites and customs which the Spanish priests found here in the religious worship of the people. They found, among other things, the worship of The Holy Virgin Mother and Child. She was worshiped as the Mother of God. The annunciation that she was to be the Mother of the Savior was made to her by an angel, and the Child became the Crucified Savior who died on the Cross. This savior fasted for forty days on a mountain and was tempted by Satan, the same as Iesa (Jesus). They found here the Sacrament of the Eucharist and Communion. They also found the institution of prayer, confession, belief in the forgiveness of sin, fasting, and the doing of penance. They found the practice of Baptism, where the infant was baptized with water and the Sign of the Cross. This water washed away sin and the child was born anew. They found the Irish institution of religious houses both for virgin women who dedicated their lives to the service of God, and for men who led a chaste and pure life. They found the Cross and Crucifix held in great veneration everywhere in Mexico, Yucatan, and in Peru. In brief, I may say that they found in practice here in America about all of the religious rites which were brought here by the ancient priests of the Irish Church of Iesa, and which were identical with what is now called Roman Catholic Christianity. They formulated this religion originally and spread it around the world to all peoples who were capable of receiving it. It is not surprising at all if, during a period of thousands of years, it became affected with some slight changes. It would be strange if it did not. Time has effected change in all religions.

Here is what the Rev. J. P. Lundy says of the rite of baptism and the manner in which it was given: "American priests were found in Mexico, beyond Darien, baptizing boys and girls a year old in the Temples at the Cross, pouring the water upon them from a small pitcher." In South America the natives took baths as a religious rite to cleanse away sin, and a very natural, but for all a remarkable, thing about it is, that the Irish name of those baths have survived for those thousands of years and have come down to us to confront and refute those despicable frauds who have stolen the fruits of the Great Irish Apostles, who were the first to preach the Gospel of "The Word" to the whole world. Those baths were called "Opacuna," or the "bath of sins," that is, the bath for the cleansing of sin. The Irish word for sin is "paca," and "pacuna" means "the sins." These facts leave no room for doubt as to whom we owe the civilization of Mexico, Yucatan, and Peru, and elsewhere on this American Continent.

A Spanish priest, the Rev. Father Acosta, in speaking of the religious rites and customs of the natives, says: "The Indians had an infinite number of other ceremonies and customs which resembled the law of Moses, and some of these which the Moors use, and some approaching near to the Law of the Gospel, as the baths of *Opacuna*, as they call them; *they did wash themselves in water to cleanse themselves from sin*" (*Bible Myths*, p. 323).

The Rev. Acosta seemed to marvel at these things, and,
as if to account for their presence among the Indians, as
he calls them, gives it as his opinion that Satan usurped
these things and gave them to the natives for his service,
as he wished to be worshiped with the things which were
used in the worship of God (*Bible Myths*, p. 404).
His opinion is just so much nonsense and was intended for
his ignorant and superstitious followers of that age.
They also found that the natives had the doctrine of the
Trinity from the Irish Sun Worship.   One of the Mexican
Divinities was Tlaloc (Talac — the Irish Sun God).   The
names of the persons of the Trinity are easily recognized
even in this our day, as Irish names of The Sun God,
namely, Yzona, — Iesona; Bacob, the genitive of
Baal; and Echia, which is but a variant of Eac, The Sun
God, with an ending added to it to formulate a name.
And with all this we find that the Mayas of Central
America worshiped the Irish Sun God Kukulcan
(Cuculan).   Can all this be attributed to mere "accidental coincidence," or can any of these be called an "isolated
fact"?   No, they belong to a series of facts constituting
a mass of evidence which establishes beyond all doubt
the racial identity of the authors of our ancient American
civilization.   It has just been announced (April 19th,
1923) that in the ruins of the City of Chichen-Itza there
has been discovered the statue of Chac Mool, the famous
Tiger King of the ancient Mayas.   This is none other
than a statue of the personified Sun God, still bearing his
ideal mythic title Chac Miol (from the Irish Cac, each,
every, all, the whole, universal).   As Iesa is the personal

Savior of each and every man, He is also the Universal
Savior of all. And Miol, an animal — any animal — is
an ideal term which the ancient Irish priests applied to
the Sun. Chac Mool is called the Tiger King because of
the fact that the tiger (jaguar), a fierce native animal,
is King of the jungle of Yucatan. This is after the Irish
ideal in our Bible, that the Sun is the Heavenly Lion, and
the earthly lion is the King of the animal world. It is
from this ideal that we get the term "Lion of the Fold of
Judah." What stronger proof could be adduced or
wished for with which to confound the falsifiers of history,
Roman or British, and those who follow their lead? In
the press news of the day is published the opinion of an
archaeologist that the date of the structure of the vast
architectural remains of Chichen-Itza goes back to the
7th century A.D. Such an opinion will bear revision in
view of the convincing evidence of a vastly greater
antiquity. Where, we may ask, can it be shown that any
other such like structures have been built in any part of
the world since the seventh century, or within even the
period, so-called, of the Christian era? No, those
buildings are many thousands of years older than some
would have us believe.

The Cross and the Crucifix are specially and peculiarly
identified with the ancient Aryan Sun Worship and
Christian Church of Iesa Chriost. They are symbolic
of the crucified Sun in the heavens and of His Human
counterpart, His Spirit in Man, in the flesh. This identification of those symbols with the ancient Irish, who
were the original missionary race of the world, makes it

easy to understand why there is such a similarity in the names of the Hindoo Savior Christna and the Christian Savior Christ. They are one and the same and came from the same source. And this explains also why Brahminism, Buddhism, and Christianity so nearly resemble each other — they are all due to those missionaries of the Irish first Church of Christ. It has always been a puzzle to honest investigators to account for this striking resemblance. If the exploits or past history of the ancient Irish people were chronicled in our histories, there would have been no difficulty whatever in accounting for those facts. The same policy of destruction, suppression, and alteration which was pursued in Ireland by Rome she also put into execution on this Western Continent. In Mexico, as elsewhere, anything that was found resembling Christianity was destroyed, if it was possible to do so. The Roman priests destroyed all the books they could find, and those they preserved they altered. "They deleted whole chapters from the writings of the native historians who wrote the history of Mexico" (*Bible Myths*, p. 199). Everything written by the natives was subject to an inquisition of the Spanish priests.

But, despite all the destruction of literature and monuments by the Spaniards and others, there is enough left to fully prove the connection between the Irish or Aryans and the discovery and settlement of this Western Continent. There is a tradition among the natives of Central America that the first of their people came from over the sea to the eastward, and were white men and bearded; and the beard has been proverbially worn by the ancient Irish, — they are so portrayed to us. And what is more, it has been found that one of the oldest of the Maya races, the Chiapenec, after the lapse of many thousands of years, has in its language many words of the same meaning and almost identical with "Hebrew." This is according to a Mexican scholar, Sr. Melgar, in "North Americans of Antiquity," p. 475 (quoted in Donnelly's *Atlantis*, p. 234). He has compiled a list of words of both languages which bears out his contention. And it has been shown, according to Donnelly, that there is a similarity between the Maya and the Phoenician alphabets, which is not surprising, in view of all the facts. When we consider that the Irish were the "Phoenicians" and also, as we have shown, that the "Hebrews" were the priestly cult among the Irish race, it makes very plain the identity of those "three peoples" as being *one and the same*. Investigators have noted the relationship between the "Hebrews" and the "Phoenicians," attributing it to the spread of Hebrew culture and influence among the latter. This seems to be as far as they have been able to go toward enlightening us. They have left us to infer that this connection was due to the two peoples occupying two adjoining sections of country, the Hebrews occupying the interior pastoral country and the Phoenicians -the seacoast. Those investigators seem to have accepted the false story of history at its face value and to have drawn their inferences accordingly. The "Phoenicians" and the "Hebrews" were one and the same race, as much so as two brothers living in the same household or father and son in the same family.' These are but "trick" names for the Irish race; Ireland was their seat, capital, and home country, not the eastern coast of the Mediterranean or Syria. This exposes a major deception of history and surely will help to give a clearer perspective of the past and a quickened realization of the fraud which has been imposed upon us. This deception has caused no end of confusion among scholars and investigators. But the announcement of the identity of those "three races" as being *one* is a fact, given out in these pages for the first time, with a positive assurance of truth. The disclosures made here will be of aid to future investigators and philologists in tracing and accounting for the changes which have been made in the three alphabets, said to have belonged respectively to the Irish, Hebrews, and Phoenicians. They are but variations of the one. We have good reason to believe, and it has been so stated, that there have been changes made in the Irish alphabet since the advent of the Latin influence of Rome into Ireland. The research work and explorations which have been made, with the excavations now going on, at the immense ruins in Mexico and Central America, if properly appraised by unbiased and capable investigators, will without a doubt correspond with the facts set forth in these pages. The very character and nature of these ruins,—Pyramids, Sphinx, and temples at Palenque near the City of Mexico and at Uxmul and Chichen-Itza in Yucatan, and others elsewhere in America — are sufficient evidence to establish the authorship of those vast, impressive, and inspiringly instructive remains. Those first religious rites and ceremonies which were found here by the Spaniards are peculiarly of Irish origin, and have been identified with their early Christian Sun Worship from the most ancient times.

The Irish were the inspired authors of Christianity, which is plainly evident from what has been unfolded herein, and their rites are still observed in the disguised Christian Sun Worship of the present day.* It all goes to show that there has been a deception practiced on the Christian people of the world, a terrible and a cruel deception. The reason for it is no longer a secret. And while those early Masters, who formulated those rites and, as well, the ethical and spiritual principles which we find embodied in the myths and allegories of our Bible, were born as Irishmen, of the Irish race, they were really for the world at large. They labored for all humanity. They carried the Divine Message of God's Truth and the Brotherhood of Man around the world, East and West, North and South, and gave freely to such as were able to receive. To those great teachers we are indebted for our culture; we owe more to them than to any other. They cannot, and they must not, be denied this acknowledgment. Their works are spread through-

* A few days ago (March 18, 1923) an Episcopal clergyman gave in his church in New York City a service and chant after the manner of the Egyptian Sun Worship, and, as reported in the press of the day, he called the attention of the congregation to the purpose which he had in giving such a service. He said it was to show "the unity of all religion." I admired his candor. If he explained anything further to his congregation, he was not so reported in the article referred to.

out the world and bear a correspondence that is unmistakable. They built on so grand and imposing a scale as to proclaim to us of today their fidelity and loyalty to their Exemplar and Ideal Savior, The Sun God, whom they conceived as the Logos and Creator of all. And in honor of Him, for His glorification and worship, they built those great and magnificent Pyramids, towers, obelisks, Sphinx, and temples. In brief, their works and ideals can be recognized everywhere, from the rock-walled temple ruins of the Angkor Wat in distant Cambodia to Siam, from Ellora and the Cave Temple of Elephanta in India to the islands of the Pacific, from Ireland to Egypt, from Syria to Peru, Yucatan, and Mexico. The character of their works cannot be mistaken.

These facts are so clear that they cannot be mistaken or set aside; they are convincing and positive proofs; they proclaim to the world that both the religious institutions and the civilization which existed on this Western Continent for thousands of years were brought here by the priests of the ancient Irish Sun Worship and religion of Iesa Chriost, The Sun God.

CHAPTER XII

THE GOING INTO EGYPT

THE Aryan Brotherhood of Magian Adepts of Ancient Eire was made up of advanced souls who were selected to be the Elder Brothers and instructors of the infant or backward races of mankind in a very early period, comparatively speaking, of human habitation in this round of evolution on this earth. They were incarnated into bodies, or born again into the flesh, to serve as guides and teachers for the new and unevolved souls who were not far enough advanced at the expiration of the previous round of planetary existence to avoid rebirth. These new souls were reincarnated here for the purpose of going through a vast series of incarnations, which are necessary to the development and growth of body, soul, or mind, and spirit power to attain perfection. The number of incarnations varies with each individual according to his progress toward spiritual perfection and the complete and final eradication of all earthly desires from his nature.

This Brotherhood of Adepts were domiciled in Eire for many thousands of years, during which time they explored nature in all its manifold and various aspects, both from within and without. It was here that they developed and acquired the vast and wonderful knowledge and science as demonstrated in the construction of

The Great Pyramid of Iesa, which has been the marvel of all ages since. They not only acquired a knowledge of physical nature but also gained a knowledge and mastery of the spiritual and God-like powers within themselves, which are latent in every man, and became the true Magicians, of which both history and tradition tell us.

The evidence that Ireland is the original home of the Aryan race and the island in which the Magian priesthood rose is overwhelming. All signs point to this country to confirm this fact. Ignatius Donnelly, in his work *Atlantis*, has produced a mass of evidence to bear out this point, although he is laboring, while doing so, with the idea of trying to prove the one-time existence of the lost continent of Atlantis as described by Plato. He accepted "Plato's" story at its face value, not realizing that this story was but a fable invented by the priests, who have written Plato's works, and intended this story to serve as an historical drop-curtain on the stage of Ireland's great career. The story was invented to veil her past and to place her in oblivion at the bottom of the "Atlantic" Ocean.

Donnelly was thoroughly convinced withal that the East or Asia was not the home of the Aryan race, and it is to be regretted that he did not become aware of the deception, as well as of the plot which inspired it, so that he could knowingly have refuted the propagandists, who have been writing spurious history, and have applied his logic and facts to Eire instead of to the fictitious "Atlantis." He quotes F. Pezron, in his *Antiquities of the Celtae*, who shows that the Celtae were the same as the

Titans, the *giant race* who rebelled in Atlantis, and "that their princes were the same with the giants of Scripture." This is clear enough to be easily understood by anyone who has not been blinded by fiction. We can see here preserved in the mythic story of the Titans an allusion to Eire's great Magian Cult. He says further that the same author states that the word Titan "is perfect Celtic, and comes from Tit, the earth, and Ten or Den, man."

We can verify the truthfulness of this definition of the word Titan. It is correct, and most suggestive and pronounced in what it reveals to us. It is further corroborative evidence pointing unmistakably to Ireland as the homeland of the Scriptures and the seat of the great Magi, and of the ancient spiritual culture and civilization. From this center they spread their culture to the ends of the earth. In the first wave of their advance, they gave Taoism (the way, a monastic order), and a later wave gave China Fo (one of the Irish names of the Sun God). He still "shines on the hills of Han."

They followed the Sun around the earth and preached the Gospel of Light and Life-everlasting and Continuous to the whole world — the Gospel of Iesa Chriost, now called Jesus Christ. It was the seed they sowed that leavened the whole lump. And it is this very fact which is confirmed by the words attributed to the bogus Roman character "St. Paul," though he remains silent as to who accomplished this arduous and wonderful missionary work which was performed thousands of years before this mythical personage (Paul — the Spirit in the Flesh) was formulated by the British priests of the Roman

Church. It is quite obvious that Paul or his supposed apostolic associates, in the few short years of their ministry, or their whole life-time for that matter, could not have done this work. He is made to say in the Epistle to the Colossians: "For the hope which is up for you in Heaven, *whereof ye heard before in the word of the truth of the Gospel which is come unto you, as it is in all the world*" (Chap. I, 5, 6).

The falsifiers of history have endeavored to show that the Aryan race originated or developed in Asia. This is plainly a trumped-up theory. We will let Mr. Donnelly speak on this point. He says: "But we have seen that in the earliest ages, before the first Armenian migration of the historical Aryans, a people went from Iberian Spain and settled in Ireland, and the language of this people, it is now admitted, is Aryan. And these Iberians were originally, according to tradition, from the West" (*Atlantis*, p. 457). That is, from Eire which lies in the Ocean to the West of Europe, as the Irish brought their colonies and culture *to Iberia* and not Iberia to Ireland, as we have been told.

Mr. Donnelly, in pursuing his inquiries, further says: "Where, we ask, could this ancient nation, which existed before Greek was Greek, Celt was Celt, Hindoo was Hindoo, or Goth was Goth, have been located? The common opinion says in Armenia or Bactria in Asia. But where in Asia could they have found a country so peaceful as to know no terms for war or bloodshed (p. 460). . . . The name of the elephant, 'the beast with a hand,' occurs only twice in the 'Rig-Veda;' a singular omission if the Aryans were from time immemorial an Asiatic race. And 'when it does occur,' according to Whitney in his 'Oriental and Linguistic Studies,' 'it is in such a way as to show that he was still an object of wonder and terror to them'" (*Atlantis*, p. 459).

So, despite all the confusion of thought on this most important point, caused by the aforesaid prevaricators of history, as to the original home of the Aryans, the truth has at last been clearly brought out. And so, it must not seem strange even to the average reader to think that the world could be for so long a time so beguiled. Our beliefs regarding objects or facts are oftentimes accepted by us unconsciously without due process of reasoning, and, in youth, we form prejudices in the mind which later are difficult to eradicate and overcome. Writers and investigators are no different from others and have to contend with these influences and overcome them if they wish to arrive at the truth. It was the result of long research which caused the author of *Atlantis* to abandon preconceived ideas and thus bring to his mind the conviction that "the fathers of the Aryan race must have dwelt for many thousand years so completely protected from barbarians and wild beasts that they at last lost all memory of them, and all words descriptive of them; and where could this have been possible save in some great, long-civilized land, surrounded by the Sea, and isolated from the attack of the savage tribes that occupied the rest of the world? And if such a great civilized nation had dwelt

for centuries in Asia, Europe, or Africa, why have not
their monuments long ago been discovered and identified? Where is the race who are their natural successors, and who must have continued to live after them
in that happy land where they knew no human and
scarcely any animal enemies? Why would any people
have altogether left such a home? Why, when their
civilization had spread to the ends of the earth, did it
cease to exist in the peaceful region where it originated?"
(*Atlantis*, p. 461.)

It is to be regretted that this great student and investigator, possessing a wonderful mind, and who had
in his day a reputation both as a writer and scholar,
did not have some inkling of the purpose and cause which
produced such great changes in the homeland of the
Aryan race, that its identity was no longer recognizable
to his mental view. Had he known of the true cause
which was back of the changes wrought, how well he
could have pointed his inquiries direct to the successors
of the Roman and Allied Marauders, the Danes and
Norse, and the later British Ally and spoliator who laid
this Aryan Motherland in ruins. However, his questions find an answer in these pages. A faint echo
of the happy state which prevailed in Eire, when she
ruled the continents and the seas and carried her culture and her commerce to the ends of the earth, has
come down to us as a tradition which has been commemorated in song by the poet Moore. The tradition
takes the form of an incident wherein a gallant knight,
who hears of a young lady purposing to make a journey

alone through the island, offers his services as an escort.
She declines his offer, relying upon the honor and up-
rightness of her countrymen to assure her safe-journey
unmolested through the island from end to end. The
poet couches her refusal of "Sir Knight" in these words:

"Though they love woman and golden store,
    Erin's sons love honor and virtue more."

The sentiment in this tradition, as expressed by
Moore, has been attributed by some as merely due to
the love of chivalry of the ancient Irish. No, this
does not rightly express it. It was all that and something else besides. It rested upon a basis of high ethical
and spiritual culture. Among them woman was re-
spected, honored, and exalted. It finds expression in
the feminine name applied to Eire by an ancient poet,
"Her name was Banba," the Good Mother, "but her
right name was Athor." (Athor means the Ether, the
primordial substance.) They raised woman to her true
position as councilor and equal. They idealized and
glorified the feminine principle in such manner that the
standard they set has been a model for other nations
since their day. Metaphorically and mystically they
made her Mother of God, Queen of Heaven, Co-Equal
with the Father.

Some would have us believe that it was in Persia that
the Magi developed and that it was Turanian instead of
Celtic. That is easily shown to be false from the fact
that the Persians got the very name of their Supreme
Deity, Zeruane Akerene, from the Irish Magi who first
introduced light and knowledge into Persia. If the

Magi had developed in Persia, they would not have had to borrow term or name in which to express Him from another cult or people. The name is Irish, or Celtic, and is but slightly modified. Zer is from the Irish Sor (bright), Ane means a circle. Hence, the Sun, the Bright Sun. Akerene is from the Celtic Keren, meaning black or dark. The Supreme God of the Persians then expresses the two opposites, or the active and passive principles in nature and is the God of Light and Darkness, implying the Sun God. This is in keeping with the Irish Magian idea, as one of their titles of the Sun God which has come to us was Talac or Dalac, the two stones, the sexes, the two opposites, light and darkness, the active and passive principles in nature.

The Persian Zoroaster lit his torch at an Irish fane, for the very name also bespeaks its origin. Zor is but a variant of Sor (bright) and Aster is from the Irish Aosar (God, the Bright God, the Sun God). So Zoroaster is the Sun God personified and is meant for the Archi-Magus or the High-Hierophant of the Sun Worship.

During their stay in Eire, the Magi developed and instructed those whom they selected to add to their number in order to form a body numerous enough to spread light and civilization to distant parts, to be sent out as missionaries and colonizers to the various other countries. Here on this island, secluded from the rest of the world at that time, they developed and maintained vast religious communities which eventually took tribal form. And here was where the patriarchal form of government first arose and here was the scene of the incidents commemorated in the Bible story written by the inspired Magi, in which were set down the precepts of the law as well as the stories told in allegorical and mythic form of incidents and human experiences gleaned within the precincts of "Inis Fail," the island of wisdom, the "Sacred Isle" of the ancient Magi of Iesa, but not of Rome.

Strange as it may seem to the uninitiated of all lands, here was where those who are referred to as the "Hebrew" cult lived and developed the arts and sciences which they spread throughout the ancient world from this their homeland. It was this order of priesthood who are secretly alluded to as the so-called "Hebrew" or Jewish race. There never was another, for it is a gross misnomer to apply it to the modern Jew, so-called, whose race has simply been made the victim of a heartless and cruel persecution in order to serve the purpose of Roman fraud. Any person who will study the Irish language or investigate the Irish tribal system and traditions and the institutions of the Druids will recognize it at once. The mantle of this great priesthood is so unique that it cannot successfully be made to fit the shoulders of any other.

These Adepts knew the Sun as their Creator, the visible representative of the Great Invisible Deity, their Savior and their Guide. They emulated Him in almost every way and worshiped Him knowingly and consciously as the poor Christian of today is led to do un-

knowingly and unconsciously under the disguised name of
the personified Jesus.   When the time became propitious
for them to begin their mission, they migrated to Egypt
in sufficient numbers to take possession of that country.
This fact is commemorated in the Bible myth of Jacob
and his family going into Egypt, and in "profane"
history, which is but a redressing of the Biblical narrative for secular use, it is alluded to as the Invasion of
Egypt by the Hyksos, or Shepherd Kings.   The name
Hyksos is a disguised form of the Irish term Tig-suas
(which is also pronounced Hig-suas), meaning Upper
House and implying the rule of the Magian Priesthood.
It is in conformity with the system of deception persistently carried out by the British and Roman priesthood in submerging all that would identify the Great
Irish Adepts with their wonderful achievements.

Those Priest Kings were called "Shepherds" in the
sense that the people they ruled over were called "flocks."
In the narrative, Philetion, their ruler, we are told, pas-
tured his flocks around the base of the Pyramid.   That
his flocks did not consist of sheep can easily be inferred
from the quite obvious fact that the region surrounding
the Pyramid is a sandy desert and could not afford pas-
turage to grazing animals of any kind, either at that
time or since.   The ancient Irish Priests constructed
their mythology in accordance with the spiritual facts
in life and in nature.   They personified and gave human
form to ideas and vitalized them so that they seemed
like real characters.   The later order of priests who
have succeeded them adopted a similar method to set

forth their fables, which have been taken as facts and accepted unquestioningly. Such is the story of Joseph, whose "brethren" sold him as a slave into Egypt. Joseph, in this incident of the Bible myth, represents the spiritual man, Ego or Self, condemned to dwell in this earthly body. His brethren who sold him were his *desires*, which still clung to his lower nature and condemned him to come back from the world of spirit again to incarnate in a new body. This myth is true to nature and to fact, for man is a moral being and will be drawn back again, life after life, into the body and will suffer all the ills and trials of earthly existence, until he resolves to conquer his desires or lower nature and live a strictly moral and spiritual life. It will be remembered that, in the story, the brethren cast Joseph into a "pit," which is but an allusion to rebirth in the body.

The ancient Irish mythologists had the idea of the triune nature of man in mind when they likened the Earth unto a woman and called her Mother Ceres (pronounced "Keres" in Irish), a name which was later accredited to the goddess who was transferred to Greece by the plagiarists. In the myth she was the spouse of the Sun. She has been represented geographically by the three grand divisions of the ancient world according to the idea of the three principles of body, soul, and spirit. Africa, from the Irish A Fear (pronounced a far), a man, represents the body or sensual nature, seed and generation; Asia, from Akolasia, passion, represents the principle of the soul or passional nature, growth and germination; Europe, from the Irish Oirp, of the East or Sun, figuratively the Highest, the Goddess, represents the Spirit.

The myth of Noah and his three sons also follows the threefold system, but it bears the plainest evidence of being altered by the English transcribers, for we find the English word "Ham" introduced to serve as the name of one of the sons. The three sons are Shem, Ham, and Japhet. Ham, the hips, as the name literally means, represents Africa, the lower or sensual nature of man, generation. Shem, from the Irish Sam, Samuin and Shemos, the Sun, represents Asia or the navel, which is said to be the region of the passional nature, germination. Japhet, from Iao (Yah, changed by using the letter *J* instead of *I* into Jah), whence we get Jah, Jahve, Yahve, Jehovah, Japhet, represents Europe, the head, spirit, or higher nature of man.

The word Africa implies inconstancy. The word is formed from two Irish words A Fear (a man) and Fraca (sport or debauch), as "afearfraca" is considered an inconstant man — sensuality. It is amazing to consider the time and energy expended by many earnest men in trying to connote facts and connect the various and fictitious "Hamitic," "Shemitic," and "Japhetic" races of men. Investigators have been following a false scent, and it would have been almost as fruitful for them to have been searching for any other imaginary races, as the Porpodaries or the Hydandarenes, for instance.

In the myth as set forth, Africa represents the hips or generative principle. The word Egypt itself rep-

resents the flesh or sex, the mother principle or birth
in the body.   The name is a formulated one ; it is formed
from the Irish word Igh, grease, the flesh or body, and
Eige, a web or womb (also eigheach, clamorous — desire), hence the Irish name Eighipt.   It is presented to
us in disguised form as Egypt, implying birth in the
body.

In both Irish myth and story, suggestive and often
direct and plain language is used, and the Bible itself,
being an Irish book originally, is proof of it.   As the
Sun was said to go down into a cave in the West at
night in the Ocean, to his daily death, His Spirit in Man
also descends into the cave of the body at generation
and birth, where it is said to be dead.   It is said that the
"Body" is death to the "Spirit," as when bodily desires are rampant and awake, spiritual ones are dor-
mant.   The more we are absorbed in the things of the
body and of the world, on this material plane, the less
we are in the things of the spirit.   This truth is embodied in the pyramid itself.   It is greater in bulk at the
base where it has contact with the earth than at any
other point, as the higher it ascends and recedes from
the earth, the less body it has until it terminates at the
point, symbolically, where matter ends and spirit be-
gins.

CHAPTER XIII

THE FOUR-PYRAMID GROUP AND SPHINX, DESIGNED AND ERECTED TO SYMBOLIZE MAN

THE Great Pyramid of Iesa is one of a group of four, namely: Iesa, the largest; Cheefren, the second in size; Mycerenes, the third in size; and Asycus, the least and lowest of the group. This group, with the Great Sphinx, forms the most important and significant group of symbols ever erected by the hand of man.

The complex nature of man has been set forth under a various enumeration or system of set principles, by different schools of thought, such as the threefold, fourfold, and sevenfold principles of man. This group of pyramids represents the fourfold system and, as symbolized by those monuments, is inclusive of the others.

The Magian Grand Architect built in accordance with this fourfold idea, which is also embodied in mythical and cryptic language in the Bible and again gives additional proof as to its origin and authorship by the inspired Irish Magian Adepts, who built for all time on a true foundation. Under this fourfold system, the body is divided into four regions or centers; namely, the region of the Head, the Heart, the Navel or Bowels, and the Genitals, each center being the seat of the active principles as comprehended in this fourfold summary of man's nature.

The theory which is most entertained is that the pyramids in general, and more particularly the group of four which symbolizes this fourfold summary of man's composition and qualities, were built as tombs for the kings who are said to have built them and whose names they are said to bear. Most of our modern paragraphers and writers have advanced this idea. The formulated names of the four pyramids were said to be the names of men who were rulers and members of a Dynasty who ruled over Egypt in successive order, as follows: Cheops, his brother Chephren, Mycerenus, and Asycus.

Cheops is said to have been possessed of the desire to build himself a great monument which would immortalize his name, a monument which would serve as a fit tomb for his body. His brother Chephren was reputed to have a similar ambition to erect a monument and tomb that would rival that of his brother. Mycerenus, the son of Cheops, is said to have been equally desirous of duplicating or surpassing the example set by his predecessors, father and uncle, and erect a monument and tomb for himself. And Asycus also, we are told, was ambitious to even excel all the others and erect an enduring monument and tomb to perpetuate his memory. The historical authenticity of this dynastic family of kingly personages has been generally accepted until now. My discoveries prove them to be allegorical and fictitious and will destroy this

fiction and substitute therefor the sublime and valuable
truths which are secretly embodied in the names of
those four pyramids. The explanation of the symbol
of the Great Sphinx will also throw additional light
on the purpose which inspired the erection of those gi-
gantic monuments and the truths which they were so
faithfully intended to convey to the initiated, and destined henceforth, we believe, to be a perpetual reminder
to man of what he now is and what he is ultimately to
become—one in union of spirit with The Sun God Iesa,
The Creator.

CHAPTER XIV

The Mystery of the Sphinx: the Problem Solved

FROM the very remote age in which this strange and peculiar monument was erected, as a companion symbol to The Great Pyramid of Iesa, it has mystified reflecting mankind.

Outside the ranks of the comparatively few who were chosen for initiation into the mystery rites of The Great Pyramid Temple, there was no knowledge extant among the great mass of mankind regarding the significance of this strange, odd, and withal uncanny piece of architecture. This ignorance of its significance and of the reason for its being, has continued among men down to this present day. The questions which came before the minds of the men of the past ages, no less than those which come before the minds of the men of our time, were: why was this structure built; who erected it; and what does it represent; what sort of minds could men be possessed of who could have expended such a vast amount of time and energy in designing and erecting such an apparently fantastic creation in stone in the midst of the solitary desolation of the sandy desert; what use or purpose could it fulfill? No solution has come down through all the ages since that far-off time that would satisfy those earnest and longing inquiries until now.

An atmosphere of awe and mystery was purposely cultivated and spread abroad among the populace, which had the effect of making it next to impossible to arrive at a true and real understanding of the creation and meaning of the Great Sphinx. Fables were invented and circulated concerning it. The people were led to believe that this curious structure represented a monster that was but a type of a race of beings which formerly inhabited the earth, but which was now extinct. One of the regular and particular purposes for which, we are told, it was erected was to function as an official quarters for the use of the pythoness or seeress from which to give forth her oracles. And that her aid and offices were sought by the people in solving the problems of daily life which were too intricate for themselves to solve; or to gratify the curious or the mystical who desired to pry into the future. Hence, the legend of "Consulting the Sphinx" which has come down to us from very early times, though long subsequent to its erection by the Magi.

For consulting the "Seeress" is an institution or practice which, in general, has survived from a very hoary antiquity. Its character varies in degree, but, in general, it was practiced by the unregenerate. There are traces of it yet visible in our own day. For this purpose there was a special room set apart by the priests and from this niche or chamber, called the adytum, she gave forth her predictions or oracles. The mystification of the ancient populaces alone has not been the only effect of ignorance of the true nature and purpose of the Great Sphinx, but it has also served to keep modern mankind in ignorance and darkness as well.

One of the fabulous stories told which has served to keep an air of mystery about the Great Sphinx is that the Oracle propounded an enigma which no one was able to solve. She asked: "What animal is it that in its infancy walked on four legs, and in its adolescent state walked on two legs, and in its old age walked on three legs?" No one could solve the problem, we are told, until Oedipus (the priest) came along and made answer that "the animal" was man, who walked on all fours in his infancy, and on two legs in his adolescence, and, with the aid of a cane, walked on three legs in his old age. Whereupon, we are told, in a rage, the Oracle flung herself on the rocks and was dashed to death. This use of the Great Sphinx was but a minor one, and, when it was inaugurated, was for the purpose of interesting and holding the multitude in subjection.

The primal cause and reason for the erection of this most unique structure, with the head of a woman and the body of a lion, was to fulfill the design of the great Irish Adept architect to form an indispensable and integral part in The Great Pyramid symbolic group and serve as a most fitting symbol of Man. He is here represented in his twofold aspect, the upper part representing the human soul nature, and the lower part the animal nature and qualities in his being.

In a most true and fitting sense, then, the Great Sphinx was designed to symbolize the unregenerate man, who has as yet two aspects only, Soul and Animal nature.

He has not yet become spiritual, spirit being the third aspect in man's triune nature. This explains why the head of the Great Sphinx is that of a woman, for the reason that the soul is said to be feminine. So this most impressive symbol is fittingly grouped and connected with the plan and purpose of the pyramidal monuments, and stands in direct contrast with The Great Pyramid of Iesa, which represents Spirit.

In one aspect, the Great Sphinx represents the neophyte, or in modern phraseology, the candidate who is to be inducted into the occult mysteries of The Great Pyramid Temple, wherein wisdom would be received which would enable him to liberate himself from his lower or animal, and build up his spiritual, body or nature. The location in the desert made a fit and appropriate setting for those wonderfully expressive symbols, and in accord with the esoteric or hidden truths embodied in them, as it was held that the world itself, or this material plane, is a desert to the spirit. And this brings home to us an appreciation of the great wisdom of that school of Irish Adept Masters, who were the first to discover and explore the profound depths of Man's inner nature. They were the first Phremasons (from Phre, the Sun) and it was in Ireland that Freemasonry first began, came into flower, and, from there, spread throughout the entire world. Ireland was the country par-excellence, and the original homeland of Freemasonry. The low plane to which it fell in England, under the sway of the bishops, may be estimated from the fact that it became associated with the coarse revelry of the alehouse and tavern. For modern Freemasonry is historically said to have had its birth in the Apple Tree Tavern in London in the year 1717. This fact reflects the very low moral status of the people of England under the care, or rather lack of it, of a self-indulgent clergy.

It is all too suggestive of the carousals of the inn where the piper played vulgar tunes, such as "The Alehouse Keeper in Great Glee," "The Banks of Cloddy," "Jack and His Bottle of Punch," and "The Bonnie Highland Laddie." In every age poets, philosophers, and sages have sung paeans of praise to Masonry, but not from a tavern. To say the least, it was not an ideal setting. for Masonry. The atmosphere of the tavern is not suitable to the Temple or to higher aspirations. Well may men exclaim : O Eire, to what depths hast thy Bright Fame fallen through the baseness and rapacity of those who envied thy glory and coveted thy possessions ! They extinguished thy light without themselves possessing it. Freemasons have accepted much for granted. In this respect they do not differ from the generality of men.

Freemasonry has lost many of its ancient landmarks, and its lights have been dimmed through the influence of the "Bishops," who have made it subordinate to the creeds. Metaphorically speaking, the Christian Creeds are but rivulets from the well, flowing through and polluted by the alluvial soil of human misconceptions. Ancient Phremasonry was the clear well of wisdom which tradition tells us was geographically situated in

Midian, — not the fictitious, so-called, Media of the priest-scribes, but what was anciently the province, now the county, of Meath in Ireland where was situated "Seiscan," the seat of wisdom at Tara. If Masonry has become materialistic or narrow and has lost her soul through the influence of priests and prelates who have obscured her light, she yet shall find it and be restored to her former glorified estate. She shall become again the bright, resplendent, and adorable, The Great Mother of all living.

The paucity of knowledge among men regarding the significance of these Great Emblems has found expression in a phrase which has become an aphorism, to wit: "As meaningless as the Pyramids and the Sphinx." The truths which are herein unfolded leave no further use for such a phrase, and, as a comparative expression of speech, it henceforth becomes redundant. For those venerable monuments once more become alive with meaning and bespeak to all men their inspired message; and as time progresses they will increase as objects of fervid interest and elicit more and more the wonder and admiration of mankind for the truths they embody and for the Great Master Adepts who in this manner memorialized them.

In its ancient perfect state the unique structure of the Great Sphinx had an outer covering of white stone and was crowned with a silver head-piece to symbolize the imperishable nature of the Soul and to reflect back those streaming rays which it received from the Lord Iesa, The Heavenly Sun (Son).

CHAPTER XV

THE PYRAMID OF ASYCUS

BACKWARD or undeveloped man born into the body or flesh in the physical world is engrossed in his animal nature, sensuality, and it may be said that the generality of mankind, even today, although the race has advanced somewhat on the upward trend, are still more or less enchained by their gross sensual nature. Therefore, in accordance with this fact in man's nature, the Pyramid of Asycus represents the lower principles or the sensual nature in man, seed and generation. The true definition of the word Pyramid will of itself at once suggest this meaning. The derivation of the word has been sought for by many writers and investigators without success. They have sought for it in the Greek, Arabic, Coptic, Latin, Spanish, and French languages, but they have never ventured to search for it at its true source. Dr. Seis, in his Pyramid work, *A Miracle in Stone* (p. 46), cites Chevalier Bunsen as authority that it is a Coptic word meaning a "division of ten," from pyr, meaning division, and met, meaning ten. However this may be, in so far as the meaning of the Coptic words pyr and met are concerned, they are not germane to the idea or sense embodied either in the word Pyramid or in the symbol itself. That it is not the true derivation of the word will be seen.

The word Pyramid has a true and faithful correspondence and relationship to what has already been explained regarding the lower principle of man's nature.
In this word we again discover the fine hand of the
clerical "doctor" at work to obscure the origin and
authorship and meaning of these grand and venerable
symbols. The word Pyramid is formed from the Irish
word Peir, meaning the buttocks or hips, and the
English word Amid, meaning literally the middle of
the hips or buttocks, the phallus, or organ of sex; and,
by changing the form of the word for deceptive purposes,
they have made it Pyramid. A great many investigators have been deceived by such trickery but the truth
will prevail in the end. It is this very idea of the besetting sin through man's lower nature which is in the
mind of the prophet Isai-ah, prophet of the Irish Sun
God Iesa, when he says, "So shall the King of Assyria
lead away the Egyptians prisoners, and the Ethiopians
captives, young and old, naked and barefoot, even with
Their Buttocks uncovered to the shame of the Egyptians"
(Is. XX : 4). To amplify this truth, if we do not suppress and conquer our desires, they will master and rule
us and become our "kings"; unless we overcome, we
shall be in bondage to our ruling desire. This is plainly
set forth in the words of Isaiah, "And the inhabitants
of this isle shall say in that day, Behold, such is our ex-
pectation, whither we flee for help to be delivered from
the *King of Assyria;* and how shall we escape?" (Is.
XX : 6).

In the ideology of the ancient Irish, the ass typified

the animal nature or unspiritual man, and, recognizing
the fact that all men are not equally evolved and occupying the same level in spiritual progress, the "white she
ass typified the man not possessed of spiritual knowledge
but capable of acquiring it" (*Egyptian and Hebrew
Symbology*, Art. Ass, by John W. Simons). The very
name Asycus, itself, suggests that this pyramid is called
after the Ass and was intended to symbolize this animal
or unspiritual quality in man, which he must eradicate
from his nature. It is plainly the burden of Isaiah's
thoughts — "That I will break the *Assyrians in my land*
and upon my mountains tread him under foot: then
shall his yoke depart from off them, and his burden
depart from off their shoulders." And again: "This
is the purpose that is purposed upon the whole earth:
and this *is the hand* that is stretched out *upon all the
nations*" (Is. XIV: 25, 26).

In the title of this Pyramid, we have a formulated
name composed of the Irish word Asal, or the English
word Ass, with the Greek ending, hence Asycus. This
pyramid is built of coarse brick, of a brownish or dull
yellowish hue, said to correspond in the Astral world
of colors to the Auric shade or hues emanating from
the sensual man. Thoughts and emotions have color
and, in the Astral world, a man's status spiritually is
cognized by the colors radiating from him. The nerve
center in the forehead from which emanates the Auric
light in colors indicates one's status on the Astral Plane.
— "If the light radiating from it is golden yellow, it is
the 'name' of the Sun; if dull red or green, it is the

'brand of the beast'" (*Apocalypse Unsealed*, by John M. Pryse, pp. 109–110). It is this fact in man's nature which forms the basis for the Christian being told, without any explanation being given to him, that his sins are written upon his forehead. In the Astral or the higher spiritual planes of nature, the disembodied soul goes to the plane corresponding to its condition, and this can even be much more easily perceived than a man's color can be distinguished on this physical plane, as to whether he is white or black, red or yellow. So it is a fact in nature that the plane in the Astral or lower spiritual world on which the Soul exists, immediately after leaving the body, is determined by the life it lived while in the body. If it is foul from evil thoughts and deeds, it will go to a low plane, corresponding to its condition where suffering and purification take place before it can ascend to a higher plane.

The Pyramid of Asycus was a constant reminder to the "instructed" of these important truths, that he might exercise his will to control his thoughts and reflect on the enormity, as well as on the penalty, of transgressing the good or moral law.

CHAPTER XVI

The Pyramid of Mycerenes

This pyramid represents the passional and desire principle in man. Physically it represents the navel or bowels, the region of the body which is said to be the seat of the passional or desire nature. Mycerenes is a name which has been formulated to embody the idea of the destructive force and effect of the emotions, appetites, passions, and desires upon the spiritual efforts of man to build up the spiritual fabric of his being by conquering his lower nature. The passional nature is tenacious and the desires are clamorous to assert themselves. They are forever gnawing, as it were, to eat away and destroy as fast as he builds up, and it is only by consciously suppressing them and keeping them in abeyance, until he is finally able to eradicate them from his nature, that spirituality is attained.

This pyramid symbolizes this fact in man's being. That such a fact is a part of man's nature becomes very plain to us when we understand that in the long ages of the past, the soul or personality of man has evolved through the animal kingdom, and he retains more or less strongly yet the traits and tendencies of the animal nature in his personality, such as anger, selfishness, jealousy, etc. This fact is embodied in the Bible myth

of the Ark; for man himself is the Ark into which went
a pair, male and female, of the animals of every living
species. So the name of this pyramid has been invented to secretly embody this principle or truth. It
is a most suggestive name when once it is explained. It
suggests that the "mice" are in us. Mice and moles
gnaw and burrow and often destroy the work of man on
the material plane; the animal passions, emotions, appetites, and desires of man gnaw and destroy and defeat
his efforts to build up his spiritual or Solar body. They
interfere with and prevent the perfecting work of man,
if they are not suppressed and overcome.

This truth is embodied in the allegorical description
of the building of the walls of "Jerusalem." This city
represents the spiritual body of man or the Heavenly
City, which is within himself. The building of this
spiritual city or body is the burden of Nehemiah's theme.
The characters, Sanballat and Tobiah, introduced in the
story, are merely derogatory epithets personified and
applied to traits and tendencies in the man who is identified with his sensual nature. And the Arabians and
Ammonites, wandering peoples of the desert of low and
thieving proclivities, are introduced to represent these
lower qualities in man. This allusion made here will
be found in the fourth chapter and seventh verse, which
is as follows: "But it came to pass that when Sanballat
and Tobiah, and the Arabians, and the Ammonites,
and the Ashdodites, heard that the walls of Jerusalem
were made up, and that the breaches began to be stopped,
then they were wroth." This will make the meaning

very clear when the name "Ashdodites" is defined. It signifies "the singed," from the Irish word Dodhe (Dothe), meaning burned — those who burn with desire, the evil doers, the sensual. And as these characters and peoples represent the lower and destructive qualities in our nature, it will be very easy to understand the meaning of the eighth or following verse in the same chapter, which is as follows: "And conspired all of them together to come and to fight against Jerusalem and to *hinder it*" (Nehemiah IV: 8).

These elements in our nature we must overcome if we would escape from the "wheel of death and rebirth." It is the goal of man to achieve liberation from his lower nature, and it is an individual task for each and every human being to accomplish. That it is an arduous task may be gleaned from the Great Magian truth, which has been preserved in the Book of Proverbs, without a note of acknowledgment by our commentators, to the Great Adepts who were the first to discover man's secret inner nature: "He that is slow to anger is better than the mighty: and he that ruleth his spirit than he that taketh a city" (Prov. XVI: 32). Hence, the Pyramid Mycerenes was erected to be a constant reminder to man to conquer his passional nature.

This pyramid in its former perfect state, like the Pyramids Chefren and Iesa, was completely covered with an outside finishing layer of white limestone, which made it an impressive object under the bright glare of the Egyptian Sun.

CHAPTER XVII

The Pyramid of Chefren

This pyramid represents physically the third region of the body or heart, which is said to be the seat of a twofold principle in man, which is commonly called the Soul. This consists of a higher and a lower principle; the former is lasting, the latter temporary and perishable. We will endeavor to show that this pyramid symbolizes this twofold principle of the Soul and that it was known to those who bestowed the name of Chefren upon it.

This is a slightly camouflaged name and is a compound Irish word with a Greek ending. The Irish word for a disembodied Soul, fairy or Ariel being, is Chefree, and, by dropping an *e* and substituting an *n* in the last syllable, they made it Chefren, which is the same as the Greek term Phren, the lower mind or perishable principle of the Soul (*The Apocalypse Unsealed*, pp. 14, 54, by John M. Pryse).

That the Irish Magian Architect who designed and supervised the erection of this Grand Pyramid, almost equal in height to that of The Great Pyramid of Iesa, understood this truth goes without saying. It was a part of the esoteric instruction which was given by them to the Initiates of all the ancient priesthoods which they established in the various countries which they visited

218

in their missionary pilgrimage. They also embodied this truth in our Irish Bible, which we have been falsely taught to believe a Syrian Jewish book. In order to grasp this truth of the dual nature of the Soul more easily (I am writing for the average reader as well as for those who may be more advanced), let us bear in mind the Neophyte who is striving to eradicate all the evil qualities and propensities from his nature and to build up his perfect Spiritual or Solar Body. In doing this work he arrives at an intermediate stage of spiritual growth, represented physically at the midriff, where he parts with his carnal or animal qualities, and which is symbolized by this pyramid.

In the upward progress of man's spiritual development, it is the first of the four pyramids emblemizing the permanent or immortal elements in his nature. The lower qualities of the Soul belong to the animal nature of man, and when he arrives at this stage of advancement, he has succeeded in separating himself from his lower principles. It is this truth which is embodied in the Bible myth of the *half tribe* of Manasseh, which is but an allusion to the Ego or Self arriving at the state of consciousness where takes place the separation of his higher mind or qualities, which are permanent, from the lower mind or perishable qualities of the Soul, which disintegrates in the lower psychic world. Manasseh is a name formed from the Irish word Man, Maon, Manas, meaning *Mind*. One of the Irish names of God is Mann, the Supreme Mind.

This truth is illustrated by "Joseph," the advancing

man who, in his upward progress, at this stage, in the
Irish myth in our Bible, is called Manasseh, and, at a
higher stage, is called Ephraim.   These two characters
are said to be brothers, which is merely a figure of speech
in the allegory (Gen. XLI: verses 50, 52). In this
story we are told that Joseph, who is the Ego or Self,
married the daughter of Potiphereh, the priest of On —
the priest of the Sun.   In the metaphor of the allegory
the daughter signifies wisdom.   So we see that Joseph
obtained *wisdom* from the *priest of the Sun*, which wisdom
enabled him to create two sons, that is, to take two progressive steps higher towards the goal of final emancipa-
tion from the trammels of his earthly nature.   This
idea of the dual character of the Soul, that no particle
of the lower principles can attach to the higher or immortal Self, is set forth in the allegory in the second chapter of Nehemiah.

In the story Jerusalem represents the ideal Holy City
or perfect Spiritual Body, which the Ego or Self is building up.   In the narrative the Ego or Self in his progress
or travels is reconnoitering the environs of Jerusalem
and the idea of this duality is secretly embodied thus:
"And I arose in the night, I and some few men with me:
neither told I any man what my God had put in my
heart to do at Jerusalem; neither was there any beast
with me, save *the beast that I rode upon*" (Neh. II: 12).
The beast is his own animal nature. And again:
"Then I went on to the gate of the fountain, and to the
King's pool: but there was no place for *the beast that
was under me to pass*" (Neh. Ch. II: 14).

So these are the spiritual truths of the Soul which are symbolized by the Pyramid of Chefren. This Grand Pyramid, before it was despoiled by zealous fanatics, had an outer casing of white limestone which glistened in the sunlight, in correspondence with the higher and immortal principle of the luminous Soul which it emblemized. This pyramid was crowned with a silver capstone. Among the ancient Irish silver was one of the precious metals sacred to the Sun Worship and dedicated to the Goddess Luna, spouse of the Sun, and typified the imperishable element of the Soul.

CHAPTER XVIII

The Great Pyramid of Iesa

An axiom of the great Irish priesthood of the Sun was that "As above, so below," but in inverse order, as for instance, what is Divine Love on the highest spiritual plane, or the celestial world, becomes carnal love here below on this physical plane. They knew by direct cognition the secrets of nature and recognized the fact that man was both spiritually and physically the child of the Sun, his Father, and of the Earth, his Mother. They venerated all life and held it sacred. As the Earth was the mother of all life, and mankind her highest offspring, they found a correspondence or analogy between the earth and the human body. As man is born on this earth through the medium of sex, they formulated a correspondence of this idea of the sex principle, which is located in the center of the body, with Egypt, which is geographically situated likewise, in the very center of the land surface of the globe (*The Pyramid of Jeezeh*, by L. McCarthy). And here in this very center of the earth's surface, they erected "an altar to God in the desert" on the bank of the river Nile, representing physically the phallus, which typified the creative power of the Sun God. It also symbolized the Spirit of God, and its regenerative power in man.

222

It was erected to be an enduring temple, a symbol and a reminder to all solicitous and wayfaring men of the significant fact that, though it is through the medium of sex that we come into earthly being, it is only through self-denial and continence and the abnegation of sex desire that the Soul of man can escape rebirth and achieve regeneration. This is the very idea embodied in the ancient Irish church service of the Mass, which has been adopted by Rome but never explained to the congregations which sit in her church pews. They are all unconscious of its true meaning and purport. Therefore, they cannot be a party to it.

- The word Mass is Irish and signifies the hips or buttocks. It is really the ancient service of the Irish celebate priesthood. It is called a "Sacrifice" or "an offering of the Mass," that is, a promise to God to sacrifice and forgo the wiles of the flesh or sex. A man cannot be wished or prayed into a spiritual state of perfection, or into Heaven, by another. It is a task which he himself must knowingly and consciously strive for and achieve. A man ignorant of these truths never obtained liberation from the flesh; that is, never became perfect and entered the higher celestial heaven. It is needless to say that the great majority of mankind is not yet ready for this step. However, it is only by knowing this great truth and following it that they will be benefited. This very idea which is secretly embodied in the ceremony of the "Mass" bespeaks most eloquently the profound spiritual wisdom of the Irish Adept Masters.

This is the great and living truth emblemized in The Great Pyramid of Iesa, which was disfigured by the Roman cohorts when they undertook to destroy all the monuments and evidence of the elder Christian Church which would conflict with the false claims set up by the Roman Church adherents.

This Great Pillar, which represented the Spirit of God in an unregenerated world and emblemized again a perfect world and a regenerated man, was defiled and desecrated, and a studied effort has ever since been made to keep the world in ignorance as to its real purpose and import and as to who its inspired builders were.

That this Great Pyramid was designed to represent the spirit in the purified or regenerated man can clearly be understood from its special and peculiar construction and the disguised and camouflaged names of "Cheops" and "Gizeh," or "Jeezeh," which have been given to it, with the idea that under these deceptive names the truth regarding it would never be suspected. In order to effect this deception they invented the word Cheops as a name for The Great Pyramid, by taking the Irish word Spoehc, or spirit, which The Great Pyramid of Iesa represents, and writing the word backwards. By this reversed form of spelling they got the word "Cheops," one of the names by which it has been designated in "history." The names "Gizeh" and "Jeezeh," which have also been applied to the "Pillar of Fire," are obtained by spelling backwards the name Hezig and Hezeej, which are but two forms of the word Iesa. These names are obtained by the use of the aspirate *h*, used in the Irish, thus Hiesa and Hezej, and by using the terminology "zig" to complete the word instead of the ending "sa." All Celtic scholars will recognize this form of the word Iesa, often carelessly pronounced as if written Iesig or Hesig.

So this crime and carefully planned deception of destroying and defacing this magnificent Temple erected to God by the Master Adepts of the Ancient Irish Church is clearly shown, and credit for its erection was denied to the most advanced cult of men that the race has ever known. This is proved so clearly that no man, whatever may have been his preconceived ideas on the subject, can ever have a doubt henceforth, despite all the subterfuge employed and misinformation given out, that this grandest and most sublime of all earth's monuments was designed by and erected under the supervision of the Irish Magi, Masters of the Sacred Science.

Physico-spiritually, the Pyramid of Iesa represents the region of the head, for here is located the brain, which is the seat of the rational intelligence. And also it contains the clusters or groups of nerve centers, which, when aroused and vitalized by the perseverance and conscious effort of the aspirant, gives him light and wisdom, through the medium of which he finally attains to spiritual perfection, or arrives at the fullness of his God-like powers. These nerve centers in man, in which this spiritual potency is slumbering, are said to be "dead" or atrophied, such as the pineal gland back of the frontal bone of the forehead. This gland, when it is awakened, becomes the spiritual eye of the Seer.

It is called by writers of occult subjects the "Third
Eye" and the "Unpaired Eye." Through it the Seer
or Adept can exercise spiritual vision at will. It becomes to such a "window into space" through which
he may, while yet in the body, cognize life and existence
in the supernal spheres. He has access to all knowledge
through the fullness of his spiritual powers. As the
soul contains all knowledge, it but remains for him to
make use of it in accordance with the Divine Plan which
he cognizes. That the Adept who built The Great
Pyramid of Iesa had reached this stage of wisdom goes
without saying, as the most sacred verities in man's
nature and attested in their Bible are faithfully embodied
in these four Pyramids. Those Irish Masters possessed
wisdom which they acquired through the development
of their spiritual powers by secret means which they
guarded securely and imparted only to those whom they
considered worthy. This can be accepted as a fact,
and will be, by every student who has the least inkling
of occult lore or experience. In what is called the
Queen's Chamber of The Great Pyramid, Prof. H. L.
Smith of Hobart College, Geneva, N. Y., discovered
evidence in a niche of that chamber which gave him,
stubborn man of physical science and all that he was,
a most profound surprise. He found two charts of the
sidereal heavens traced in the walls of this niche in the
Queen's Chamber. One of the charts represented the
sidereal year of the heavens from the time that the Pole
Star was last visible and in direct line from the shaft
of The Great Pyramid through its opening on the north

side; and the other chart was of the sidereal year preceding it. He took the trouble and labor to work out all the calculations in the problem before him to test the accuracy of those ancient charts of the heavens. He found them absolutely correct. According to Becket, the earth travels around the Pole of the Ecliptic in the period of 25,827 years. He found that the heavens were charted correctly for a period indicating more than 51,000 years. He evidently was amazed at discovering proof of such profound knowledge on the part of the builder. In a private letter, in speaking of the evidence he found there, Professor Smith says: "Either there is proof in that chamber of supernatural inspiration granted to the architect, or that primeval official possessed, without inspiration in an age of absolute scientific ignorance 4000 years ago, scientific knowledge equal to, if not surpassing, that of the present highly developed state of science in the modern world" (L. McCarthy's *Pyramid of Jeezeh*).

As the burden and fruit of our Irish Bible Myths is the production, conception, and birth of the perfect Man-God from the Earth-Man, or Belly-Man, Potipher in the sacred myth, and Firbolg, Belly-Man or Bag-Man in the Irish profane "history," so likewise is this same truth embodied in this symbolical four-pyramid group and sphinx, the highest and greatest of which typifies the ideal Perfect Man-God Iesa, the glory of the ages and of all time. This correspondence between the Bible and those symbols is a most significant fact which cannot be overlooked or set aside. It only speaks in a

more unmistakable manner of the perfidy of the two
arch-conspirators to deny to Ireland the credit for the
achievement of her men of genius. This same truth
is preserved in the cryptic writings of the fabulous historian Diodorus Siculus, who tells us that Philitis erected
The Great Pyramid. The name Philition is also applied to the Builder of this Pyramid. These are but
two forms of the same word and are meant to distinguish
the same person (the Ego or Self) at two different stages
of spiritual growth. "Philitis" is the lower man, or,
as the name implies, "the man of the blood," and at
the beginning of his development. "Philition," supposed to be a prince, is the same man who has reached
the highest stage of spiritual development, or, in other
words, under the title of Philition, the Ego or Self is
said to have erected the Perfect Pyramid of Iesa, the
symbol of the Solar or Spiritual Body. The name
Philitis is adapted from the Irish word Fuil, the blood,
but the spelling and form "Philitis" obscures it just
enough to deceive, which it was intended to do. As
it is the lower man, yet tainted with the qualities inherent in the blood, who must make the beginning to
live a better life and aspire to the things of the Spirit,
it is only natural to the system of the Irish myth makers
to give Man in this stage in the cryptic story the name
Filitis, but it was slightly changed for the purpose of
obscuring it by their successors. Those names, which
are used to indicate supposedly historic personages by
the priest-scribes who have written those histories of
the ancient past under fictitious names, such as "Dio-

dorous Siculus," etc., are simply formulated names composed to express the ideas which they wished to set forth
and are not the names of any particular individuals
who had acted a part in life.   They are mythical names
and convey no idea of the sense of true history.   Of
such characters also are all the invented names of the
ancient Egyptian dynasties which are mentioned in our
histories, so far as any particular individual king is
concerned.   But all through the mythical story are
preserved secretly allusions to facts which are contained
in those names and required only knowledge of the in-
terpretative key to be understood.

Whatever there was of real and actual history of mankind chronicled up to the time of the destruction of the
Alexandrian libraries, through the mad ambition of
Rome to reduce the world to ignorance and to rule all
mankind under her own church dominion, was destroyed.
The other great libraries that remained were those in
Ireland, which she destroyed at the time of the English
invasion.   At the time of the Spanish invasion of
America her priests destroyed all the literature which
they could find.   Any of it they spared, they altered to
suit their purpose of deception.   Wherever any writings
could be found that would shed light on the past, they
were seized and destroyed.   It is only since the conquest of the Irish Church of Iesa that the staffs of priests
were set to work by Rome to compose histories which
would furnish a proper setting or background for her
false pretensions.   At the time of the conquest of the
Irish Church and Papacy, she took over the Irish sacred

writings and mythical lore, and our Bible is an eloquent witness to substantiate my statement. She has adopted them as her own and altered them to suit her claims.

The evidence of the Irish occupation in Egypt is established by those Great Pyramids, and other monuments and remains along the Nile Valley. This fact is amply born out in secret in the mythical names given of Temples and places and of Egypt's first ruler. We are told that the founder of the first colony in Egypt was Isis, that she was worshiped there by her devotees and disciples. She is the ancient Irish Goddess or Mother of God, and the Irish introduced her worship there. At one time her worship extended all over Europe. Mythically she is the Moon, and the Night, the consort of the Sun, and she is the Ether, the primordial substance. Mystically she is the Queen of Heaven and the Mother of God, co-equal with the Father. The name is formed from the Irish Ise-Isis, meaning She, Herself, who, with Ti, He, Himself, constitutes the co-equal Father-Mother God.

The dynasty of the Pharaohs is a mythical one, and is Irish lore preserved in the Bible. The name Pharaoh has a cryptic meaning and alludes to man's peculiar composition and tendencies. The "Pharaohs" are invented rulers or personages formulated to express the idea of a stage in the allegorical story of man's generation in the fleshly body, which is a prelude to his progressive advance into the spiritual body. The name is composed of two words made into one, but slightly changed so that it might not be so easily discovered by those for whom it was not intended, that is, all outside the ranks of the priesthood. It is derived from the Irish words Fear (Far) meaning man, and Raodh, meaning to ride — the sensual man. This is the leading sense meant to be conveyed by the term and this idea is expressed in the myth, in the incident of Pharaoh's wife becoming enamored of Joseph. It also expresses the dual sex nature of man, from the word Raon, with the letter *n* omitted, meaning "both" or the two sexes. For it is a fact in nature that man is double sexed. While spirit is sexless, man born into the body is subject to the incident of being born either into a male or female body according to the lessons or experience from which his Soul or Ego is destined to gain knowledge or wisdom in each particular incarnation, until the Ego is through with the attractions of the earthly existence and completes the building of the spiritual body. This glorified body is typified by the Resurrected Savior Iesa, and emblemized by The Great Pyramid, which is the symbol of the Solar Body of man. So Pharaoh is the sensual and double-sexed, male-female man.

There is a play made with some of the names which the Irish myth-makers gave to some of their Egyptian characters, such as Potiphereh and Potipher. The name is from Poti, meaning the bowels or belly, and Pher, meaning man; but this latter half of the name has the syllable *eh* added to it, making it signify truth or wisdom. Hence, Potiphereh, we find, is the Priest of On, The Sun, the man of truth and wisdom, and the father-in-law of Joseph, who is the striving and upright spirit in man (Gen.

XLI: 45). Potipher is the lower man, as explained.
What Irishman who speaks his language will fail to
understand the metaphorical expression "fear 'n po-
toga"? It is a common expression among the Irish
to this day, the very idiom used by the Ancient Irish
Mythologists and mystics in veiling their spiritual wisdom from the uninitiated and profane. Potipher has
been enthroned in "regular order" in the line of Egyptian kings by British writers. And in our own country
his standing as a Royalty has never been seriously
challenged. The same may be said of the writers of all
the other so-called enlightened countries. It may
seem rather hard to some minds, who love fiction, to
expose him, but it is done only to introduce him in his
proper character and place in the drama of human life
and the evolution of the spirit in man. In doing this,
a real and true revelation and interpretation of truth
is given to all earnest and right-thinking men and
women whose minds have been perplexed as to the significance or reality of such personages as the Pharaohs.

Another fictitious personage is King Menes, who is
said to have founded the first dynasty in Egypt. The
revisionists have here introduced a supposedly Greek
word as a name for this mythical king. He is but a
phase of our human nature personified, and is introduced
in the allegorical story to represent the female menses.
The word "mene" is derived from the Irish word Me,
or the Greek word Men, and signifies month or monthly.
We are told in the story of Egypt that King Menes
caused a channel to be dug, leading from the River

Nile, causing water to flow under the Pyramid. This is but a cryptic allusion to this fact as explained. The River "Nile" is the blood, which circulates through the human body, and it is but a secret allusion to this fundamental aspect of man's sexual nature that "King Menes" represents. Thus he founded the first dynasty in Egypt. The word Nile is Irish and is the genitive of Fuil, blood. Inflected, the word becomes n'uil, hence Nile.

Through the splendid imagery of those ancient Irish Adepts, poets, and sages, they have given us an allegory, which is built upon the natural physical features of Egypt, and also in correspondence with the true aspects of human life. They saw in the great river of Egypt, which gave life and fertility to that country, an analogy to the "river" of blood circulating through and giving life to the human body. But it required Roman and British clerical writers to circulate the Irish Bible myth as a real and authentic history which has consistently deceived mankind up to this day.

In its ancient perfect form The Great Pyramid of Iesa had an outside covering of white stone and was crowned with a capstone of Gold, the sacred metal which was dedicated to the use of the Lord Sun, and Savior Iesa.

CHAPTER XIX

CONCLUSION

In the foregoing pages, I have endeavored to disclose who built The Great Pyramid of Iesa, and the purpose for which it was erected, a purpose and a reason which is perhaps as urgent and needful for the moral and spiritual uplift of mankind today as ever before. In the remote past its message and significance was apprised only by the comparative few. It has been my endeavor to make these most essential truths available to the many who, in the present state of enlightenment, are ready to receive them. To further this purpose, what nobler project could be the object of an international commission than the restoration of the Ancient Pillar to its pristine grandeur with its exterior casing of white limestone and its golden capstone reflecting back to Heaven its shining rays, bespeaking a perfect union of Earth and Heaven, and of the Perfect Man with his Creator.

And the Pyramid of Chefren should also be restored to its former condition with its white casing and its silver capstone which symbolizes physically the lesser light of the Moon, and spiritually the glory of the imperishable element of the immortal Soul. The two other pyramids of the group, with the Great Sphinx, should

234

also be put into as good a state of repair as will insure their preservation, for this fourfold group and Sphinx so perfectly symbolize man, that they may again, as in ages past, proclaim their immortal message to all mankind in a manner most unmistakable and impressive. They should not be allowed to perish.

This most worthy object would be a common ground upon which the enlightened representatives of all nations could meet in perfect agreement. The lessons of truth to be taught and gleaned from those monuments would do more to bring understanding and brotherhood and "Peace on earth, good will to men" than any movement yet undertaken. It would make it possible to visualize again, as of yore, before the minds of men a beacon of light in the "desert" of human life, which would make manifest to the senses, and be in consonance with the declaration of the inspired Prophet of Iesa: "In that day shall there be an altar to the Lord in the midst of the land of Egypt, and a pillar at the border thereof to the Lord. And it shall be for a sign and a witness unto the Lord of Hosts in the land of Egypt" (Is. XIX : 19, 20).

Let the restoration of this Great Altar, Sign and Witness, and Symbolic Group be an "offering" by the nations unto the Lord that they may be a perpetual reminder and landmark whose message may serve as an unerring spiritual guidance to all mankind, as bequeathed to us by the Great Ancient Irish Magian Priests of Iesa.

Printed in the USA
CPSIA information can be obtained
at www.ICGtesting.com
LVHW071119240224
772723LV00004B/244